F-16 Falcon Still in the Fight

Welcome

The people marketing fighter planes built in France delight in explaining their aircraft's extensive combat experience and export success. Both are proven. Those in Sweden take great satisfaction from explaining the design success of their jet. The Swedish jet is facing a small order book. And their counterparts in Germany love to discuss how they are building aircraft and developing extensive future capabilities. The German jet is also facing a dwindling order book.

The people working for Lockheed Martin, on the other hand, don't know what to holler about first. They've already built thousands of F-16s in Fort Worth, Texas. They're still building F-16s albeit now in South Carolina. They're set to continue building F-16s.

The F-16 was the first fighter capable of pulling 9g 'right off the runway'. Its design is pleasing to the eye. Its performance, when slick, is eye watering. Its capabilities are – in every sense – truly multi-role. It performs every modern tactical combat mission. It's been in production for over 47 years and has been involved in all the major conflicts of our time.

Designed by General Dynamics, the prototype YF-16, serial number 72-1567, was flown for the first time by Phil Oestricher at Edwards Air Force Base, California on February 2, 1974.

The first production Block 1 F-16A for the US Air Force, serial number 78-0001, was delivered to Edwards on September 6, 1978. The US Air Force took delivery of 2,231 Fighting Falcons the last of which, Block 50 F-16C serial number 01-7053, was delivered to Shaw Air Force Base on March 25, 2005 – 9,698 days later.

Twenty-five nations currently operate the F-16, with two more awaiting delivery of their first aircraft: Bulgaria and Slovakia.

The US Air Force has the largest fleet, with dozens of aircraft deployed and is operating with America's coalition partners conducting dangerous missions taking the fight to their foes.

There have been many developments since the original edition of this publication hit the newsstands in 2015. They include the Viper avionics upgrade, the latest Block 70, integration of the APG-83 AESA radar and the advent of the Have Glass series of low-observable paint schemes. All these topics and many more are contained inside this edition.

After a 47-plus year history, the F-16 remains the most prolific fighter aircraft of its generation, combat proven, affordable, and still in the race for fighter aircraft competitions around the world – a very capable aircraft, born and raised in Texas.

Mark Ayton

US Air Force/Kyle Brasier

CONTENTS

US Air Force/Captain Michael Balserak

006
Searching, Shooting, Striking
Radars, systems, and weapons – David C Isby and Mark Ayton examine the combat edge of the F-16.

018
APG-83 Scalable Agile Beam Radar
Mark Ayton runs the rule over Northrop Grumman's APG-83 AESA radar – built for the F-16.

024
Have Glass: Making the F-16 Less Detectable
Jon Lake gives the technical lowdown on Have Glass – real fancy paint for the F-16.

028
Propulsion
Chris Kjelgaard examines two engines – a modern classic and one with a bright future.

032
The Viper Upgrade
Viper – an avionics upgrade package at the heart of the latest F-16 retrofitted configuration.

038
Block 70
An overview of the Block 70 and the route taken to get there – an advanced F-16.

046
Moving to Greenville
When F-16 production moved from Fort Worth to Greenville, South Carolina it created a number of challenges. But everything seems rosy in the jet's new home.

052
X-62A VISTA
Scott Dworkin and Mark Ayton describe Calspan's X-62A in-flight simulator – doing the impossible.

062
Follow-me
Air Combat Command's 16th Weapons Squadron – instructing the art of integration.

066
Arpeccop
Always the bad guys. Air Combat Command's 64th Aggressor Squadron – playing MiG for the US Air Force.

072
Warhawks
Mark Ayton examines F-16 pilot training at Holloman Air Force Base, New Mexico.

082
Florida Makos
F-16 operations with Air Force Reserve Command's 93rd Fighter Squadron based at Homestead Air Reserve Base, Florida.

090
Mile High Militia
Colorado Air National Guard's 140th Wing – on worldwide operations.

F-16 Falcon Still in the Fight

Lockheed Martin

ISBN: 978 1 80282 746 0
Editor: Mark Ayton
Senior editor, specials: Roger Mortimer
Email: roger.mortimer@keypublishing.com
Cover design: Dan Jarman
Design: SJmagic DESIGN SERVICES, India, and Dave Robson
Advertising Sales Manager: Brodie Baxter
Email: brodie.baxter@keypublishing.com
Tel: 01780 755131
Advertising Production: Debi McGowan
Email: debi.mcgowan@keypublishing.com

SUBSCRIPTION/MAIL ORDER
Key Publishing Ltd, PO Box 300, Stamford, Lincs, PE9 1NA
Tel: 01780 480404
Subscriptions email: subs@keypublishing.com
Mail Order email: orders@keypublishing.com
Website: www.keypublishing.com/shop

PUBLISHING
Group CEO: Adrian Cox
Publisher, Books and Bookazines: Jonathan Jackson
Published by
Key Publishing Ltd, PO Box 100, Stamford, Lincs, PE9 1XQ
Tel: 01780 755131
Website: www.keypublishing.com

PRINTING
Precision Colour Printing Ltd, Haldane, Halesfield 1, Telford, Shropshire. TF7 4QQ

DISTRIBUTION
Seymour Distribution Ltd, 2 Poultry Avenue, London, EC1A 9PU
Enquiries Line: 02074 294000.

We are unable to guarantee the bonafides of any of our advertisers. Readers are strongly recommended to take their own precautions before parting with any information or item of value, including, but not limited to money, manuscripts, photographs, or personal information in response to any advertisements within this publication.

© Key Publishing Ltd 2023
All rights reserved. No part of this magazine may be reproduced or transmitted in any form by any means, electronic or mechanical, including photocopying, recording or by any information storage and retrieval system, without prior permission in writing from the copyright owner. Multiple copying of the contents of the magazine without prior written approval is not permitted.

098 Swamp Foxes
South Carolina Air National Guard's 169th Fighter Wing – the longest serving F-16 unit in the Guard.

104 Atacama Falcons
Santiago Rivas reports from Chile – home of South America's largest Fighting Falcon fleet.

110 Zeus
Greece – Ian Harding reports from the defender of NATO's southern flank and a massive F-16 operator.

116 Desert Falcons
The United Arab Emirates – the world's only Block 60 F-16 operator by Jon Lake.

126 Japan's Hybrid F-16
Dave C Isby provides an overview of Japan's F-16 derivative – the Mitsubishi F-2 fighter.

US Air Force/MSgt Jason Rolfe

F-16 Falcon Still in the Fight

Searching... Shooting...

Striking

and BVR engagements – including the use of a data link.

This new capability means the pilot can take full advantage of the aerodynamic performance of the AIM-9X. The ongoing test programme, which was nearing completion at the end of 2013, demonstrated excellent results: 17 kills for 21 test shots.

Later Block AIM-9Xs incorporate a reprogrammable computer to adjust for new IR countermeasure challenges.

The AIM-9X missile is 119 inches (3.02m) long, weighs 188lb (85kg), has a 5-inch (127mm) diameter and wings and fins with spans of 13.9 inches and 17.5 inches (353mm and 444mm) respectively.

AIM-120 ADVANCED MEDIUM RANGE AIR-TO-AIR MISSILE (AMRAAM)

The F-16's primary air-to-air weapon is the Raytheon AIM-120 AMRAAM beyond visual range (BVR) radar-guided missile.

The AIM-120 has four fixed mid-body-mounted wings, four electric motor-driven movable tail fins and an umbilical connection enabling communication with the aircraft for targeting and initialisation.

The missile consists of four sections: guidance, armament, propulsion and control.

The hardware and software necessary for target acquisition and tracking, navigation, data link processing and electrical power distribution is fitted in the guidance section.

Seeker/servo electronics, a transmitter/electrical conversion unit (ECU), an electronics unit, an inertial reference unit (IRU) and a quad/target detection device (QTDD) are also housed in the guidance section. Antennas for the QTDD are mounted in the aft portion of the guidance section.

AMRAAM uses a radar proximity fuse which activates the high-explosive fragmentation warhead at a preset distance from the target.

The missile is configured with a single boost-sustain, reduced-smoke hydroxyl-terminated polybutadiene solid propellant encased in an insulated steel case, which is an integral part of the airframe.

Control electronics, actuator batteries and four independently-controlled servo-actuators are the main components of the control section.

The latest version of the AMRAAM, the AIM-120D, was developed to add new capabilities to the AIM-120C7. Two-way data link, GPS navigation, increased electronic protection and improved range make the AIM-120D the most advanced air-to-air weapon in service today.

The AIM-120D has improved kinematics due to a longer battery life and so runs for longer, high off-boresight capability because of improved algorithms that control the flight trajectory more accurately as it hones in on the target, GPS for better accuracy as it gets further along its trajectory and a two-way data link.

Operational test (OT) of the AIM-120D finished in 2014 followed by fielding authorisations from the US Air Force and the US Navy in January 2015. Raytheon continues to ship D-model missiles to US Air Force and US Navy units.

Performance results from the OT remain classified but those deemed the most impressive are believed to include the improved trajectory during the missile's terminal stage when approaching its target and a greater range to target gained from the extended battery life and the improved trajectory.

According to a Raytheon spokesman, the company has established an AMRAAM road map with the US Air Force comprising regular software improvements designed to counter future air-to-air threats.

The AIM-120C missile is 144 inches (3.70m) long, weighs 356lb (161kg), has a 7-inch (180mm) diameter, has wings and fins with spans of 17.5 inches (444mm) respectively and a blast-fragmentation warhead of 45lb (20kg).

AIM-120C Raytheon

PYTHON AIR-TO-AIR MISSILE

Rafael Zephyr and Python are, respectively, Israeli and export designations for a family of infrared-guided (IR) air-to-air missiles.

The first version, called the Python 3, was developed from the 1970s-era Shafrir 1 and Shafrir 2 missiles. The Python 3 saw its first combat use in the 1982 Lebanon War and scored more than 30 victories against Syrian aircraft.

The Python 4 replaced the Python 3 as the standard Israeli IR-guided air-to-air missile in the late 1990s. It has a range of 15km (8.1nm).

Currently the most advanced standard air-to-air missile in operation with the Israeli Air Force is the Python 5. It uses the same fuselage, inertial navigation system, rocket motor, warhead and proximity fuse as the Python 4 but features upgraded software, an

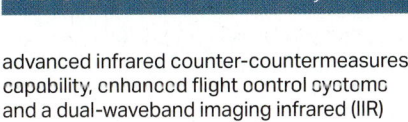
PYTHON 5 Rafael Advanced Defense Systems

advanced infrared counter-countermeasures capability, enhanced flight control systems and a dual-waveband imaging infrared (IIR) seeker.

Lock-on-before launch and lock-on-after launch (LOAL) modes give the missile an enhanced capability. In LOAL mode, target information is transmitted from the launch aircraft to the missile to enable target acquisition well off-boresight.

The Python 5 entered operational service in 2005 and gained media attention in 2012 when two F-16I Sufas shot down a UAV that had entered Israeli airspace.

The Python 5 is 3.1m (122 inches) long, has a wingspan of 640mm (25 inches), a diameter of 160mm (6 inches), a range of more than 20km (10.7nm) and a maximum speed of Mach 4. Its Derby radar-guided export version weighs 128kg (231lb), including a 23kg (50lb) warhead.

F-16 users: Chile, Israel, Singapore, Thailand, Turkey, Venezuela.

IRIS-T AIR-TO-AIR MISSILE

The Diehl BGT Defence IRIS-T (Infra-Red Imaging System – Tail control) air-to-air missile was developed by a multinational European team and intended to replace the Raytheon AIM-9L/AIM-9M Sidewinder. It entered production in 2004.

The IRIS-T has a reported top speed of Mach 3, a range of about 25km (13.4nm) and more agility than its predecessors. Other features include the ability to engage a target at high off-boresight angles and LOAL operating modes.

The complete IRIS-T capability (which has been incrementally introduced) includes compatibility with various types of helmet-mounted sights.

These capabilities have been revolutionary in expanding the lethal envelope of infrared-guided missiles. The IRIS-T has reportedly been able to turn at 60g and engage targets behind the launch aircraft. Its signal processor enables it to reject infrared countermeasures such as flares.

The IRIS-T was integrated with the F-16 following a flight test programme at Edwards Air Force Base in California during 2005. The missile's integration was enabled by the M4 OFP software upgrade introduced between 2005 and 2007.

Norway was the first F-16 operator to field the IRIS-T. The Royal Norwegian Air Force adopted AIM-2000 as its designation and used the missile in conjunction with Boeing's Joint Helmet-Mounted Cueing System.

F-16 users: Greece, Norway.

AGM-65 MAVERICK

The AGM-65 Maverick is an air-to-ground missile designed for close air support, air interdiction and suppression of enemy air defences with a lock-on before launch day/night capability.

A Maverick missile consists of three sections: a guidance package, warhead and rocket motor. The Maverick can be fitted with three different seekers: electro-optical (AGM-65B), imaging infrared (AGM-65D) and laser (AGM-65E). It can be armed with either a 125lb (56kg) shape-charged warhead with a contact fuse or a 300lb (136kg) penetrator with a delayed-fuse. The solid-rocket motor is common to all variants.

The AGM-65 has a cylindrical body, long-chord delta wings and tail control surfaces.

The AGM-65 is 97.7 inches (2.48m) long and has a fuselage diameter of 12 inches (305mm). The AGM-65B weighs 462lb (209kg), the AGM-65D 485lb (220kg) both weights include the 125lb shaped-charge warhead, and the AGM-65E weighs 628lb (285kg) including a 300lb penetrator warhead.

AGM-88 HIGH-SPEED ANTI-RADIATION MISSILE (HARM)

The AGM-88 HARM is a supersonic air-to-ground missile designed to seek and destroy enemy radar-equipped air defence systems.

This includes emissions from surface-to-air missiles, radar gathered anti-aircraft artillery and any type of radar or electronic waveform.

It is equipped with an inertial and GPS guidance system that homes in on radar emissions through a fixed antenna and seeker head in the missile nose.

A HARM missile consists of four sections: a passive broadband radio frequency guidance section; a direct fragmentation, variable charge-to-metal warhead; an electro-mechanical wing control sections; and a smokeless, solid-propellant, dual-thrust rocket motor.

The US Air Force primarily uses the AGM-88C but Raytheon is currently producing the HARM Control

F-16 Falcon Still in the Fight

AGM-88 HARM TSgt Michael Ammons/US Air Force

AGM-65 Maverick Raytheon

Section Modification (HCSM) which incorporates a GPS/INS digital flight computer for precision targeting. If an emitter shuts down, an HCSM-equipped HARM can continue to the target using the GPS co-ordinates – this overcomes a targeting issue faced by legacy missiles that only guide on emissions from the target threat.

The HCSM is retro fitted to existing AGM-88C missiles by Raytheon. The modification involves removal of the original control section and installation of a GPS/INS digital flight computer, and new software to transform the old missile into a precision-guided AGM-88F. The original seeker, guidance section (located in the front of the missile) and the solid-propellant, dual-thrust rocket motor remain unchanged.

The modified HARM also allows the pilot to designate a missile impact zone, zones of exclusion and zones in which the missile must not fly. Bill Reaves senior manager for business development SEAD/DEAD told *AirForces Monthly*: "In a nutshell it allows the pilot more control of the missile impact point, where it can hit and where it can't hit, which reduces the likelihood of collateral damage and any potential for fratricide, and provides the ability to counter target shut-down."

The AGM-88 is 164 inches (4.16m) long, has a fuselage diameter of 10 inches (254mm), and weighs 780-810lb (354-528kg) including a 143.5lb (65kg) warhead.

AGM-142 POPEYE

The Rafael Popeye air-to-surface missile was developed by Israel (with US funding) in the late 1970s and early 1980s. It was intended to be the follow-on to the first-generation US-built Walleye precision-guided munition which Israel received in 1973.

The Popeye uses an electro-optical/infrared seeker head and man-in-the loop guidance, enabled by a data link feed of the seeker's TV footage shown on a cockpit display.

The missile has a range of 80km (43.5nm) and weighs 1,360kg (3,000lb), including a 350kg (770lb) unitary warhead.

Rafael started development of the Popeye 2 Have Lite version in the 1980s. It features miniaturised and lighter electronics, improved guidance algorithms and a shorter rocket motor to reduce its weight to 1,130kg (2,500lb). It has the same warhead as the original Popeye missile and a comparable maximum range.

A pod-mounted data link feeds the seeker's TV footage to the pilot's head-up display, a capability which meant it could be used by single-seat fighters.

The Popeye 2 first flew around 1994 and entered Israeli Air Force service in 2005. An F-16 can carry two.

AGM-88 HARM Raytheon

F-16 users: Israel, Republic of Korea and Turkey.

AGM-154 JOINT STAND-OFF WEAPON (JSOW)

The AGM-154 Joint Stand-Off Weapon (JSOW) is a 1,000lb-class low-observable INS/GPS-guided family of air-to-surface glide weapons with all-weather, day/night capability.

It consists of a common airframe and avionics providing for a modular payload assembly to attack stationary or moving targets.

Once released the JSOW is an unpowered glide bomb with a range from 15 to 60-plus miles (24 to 96-plus km) – which enables the attacking aircraft to remain outside the range of point and short-range air defence systems.

The AGM-154A carries 145 BLU-97 combined effects

AGM-142 POPEYE Rafael Advanced Defense Systems

munitions for deployment against area targets such as troops, vehicles and SAM sites using GPS-aided inertial guidance.

After launch, folding wings extend and the weapon flies a pre-programmed flight path before dispensing its payload over the intended target.

The AGM-154C version features an infrared terminal seeker and carries a 500lb (227kg) two-stage Broach penetrator warhead to attack hardened targets.

JSOW-C1 has an autonomous target acquisition (ATA) capability, a Link 16 data link to enable moving target (land and maritime) strike capability.

The AGM-154 is 160 inches (4.06m) long, has a fuselage diameter of 13 inches (330mm), a wingspan of 106 inches (2.69m) and weighs 1,065lb (483kg).

GBU-12 PAVEWAY II LASER-GUIDED BOMB

The GBU-12 Paveway II is a 500lb (227Kg) laser-guided bomb which uses the Mk82/BLU-111 blast fragmentation warhead. It has large guidance fins attached to the front of the high-explosive bomb body and folding wings (the air foil group) which open on release for stability and increased manoeuvrability.

When dropped, the GBU-12's nose-mounted semi-active laser seeker tracks the laser spot on the target provided by the F-16's targeting pod, a forward air controller or an unmanned air vehicle. During flight the bomb fins move to ensure accurate impact on the target.

The Paveway II has 'bang-bang mode guidance'.

The GBU-12 is 131 inches (3.32m) long, weighs 606lb (275kg), has a warhead diameter of 10.75 inches (273mm) and an airfoil diameter of 18 inches (457mm).

GBU-10 PAVEWAY II LASER-GUIDED BOMB

The GBU-10 Paveway II is a 2,000lb (907Kg) laser-guided bomb that uses the Mk84/BLU-117 blast fragmentation warhead.

The GBU-10 is 169.9 inches (4.31m) long, weighs 2,110lb (957kg), has a warhead diameter of 10.75 inches (273mm) and a diameter of 18 inches (457mm).

F-16 Falcon Still in the Fight

Jim Hasletine

At this point the missile has acquired its spatial position and flies to the first pre-loaded waypoint at the pre-programmed altitude and air speed. A missile can be pre-programmed with eight profiles with up to 100 waypoints each. An F-16 can carry four MALD-Js.

Its decoy mode of operation is used for saturation and deception. A multiple release is employed to overwhelm operators of air defence system radar while the release of one or two missiles will appear like a fighter jet on an adversary's radar screen. The intent is to deceive the adversary into concentrating its assets into a pointless engagement. MALD-J achieves this thanks to the Signature Augmentation System (SAS) which uses active radar enhancers operating across a broad range of frequencies that enable it to mimic the radar signature of various combat aircraft.

The ADM-160C MALD-J passed operational test on the B-52H and F-16 in April and has moved from low-rate initial production to full-rate production. Raytheon delivered the 1,000th MALD in May 2014, and signed a contract in March 2015 for production Lot 8 which was part of a two-year agreement. The company is now negotiating a three-year multi-lot deal.

The ADM-160C measures 113 inches (2.87m) long, has an 11 inch (279mm) wide fuselage, a wingspan of 67 inches (1.70m) and weighs 282lb (127kg). **David Isby, Ian Harding and Mark Ayton**

APG-83
Scalable Agile Beam Radar

Mark Ayton provides an overview of the Northrop Grumman APG-83 Scalable Agile Beam Radar.

F-16 Falcon Still in the Fight

Northrop Grumman's APG-83 Scalable Agile Beam Radar (SABR) is defined as a multifunction, active electronically scanned array radar. It was developed as the replacement radar system for the legacy APG-68 type installed on countless US Air Force F-16 aircraft for the Radar Modernization Program (RMP). According to the US government's Director of Operational Test and Evaluation (DOT&E) the APG-83 provides F-16 pilots with air-to-air and air-to-ground situational awareness, high-resolution synthetic aperture radar mapping, fire control, and datalink support to air-to-air missiles. F-16 pilots use the APG-83 with onboard weapons, to accomplish the full kill chain against air, ground, and surface targets, from beyond visual range and in all weather conditions. Compared to the legacy APG-68 system, the APG-83 enables targeting and engagement from greater ranges with enhanced accuracy and combat identification.

According to Northrop Grumman the APG-83 can operate in dense electronic environments and can conduct simultaneous multi-mode operations. The radar unit is designed for installation as a form, fit and function modification that operates within the F-16's existing forward fuselage space, with the original power and cooling capabilities without making any major modifications to the jet.

Northrop Grumman developed a liquid cooling system for the APG-83 which allowed Lockheed Martin to retain the same environmental cooling system used for the mechanically scanned radars fitted to earlier Block F-16 aircraft.

Implementation of the RMP seeks to extend the operational viability and reliability of the F-16 and provides pilots with increased bandwidth that allows the aircraft to detect, track and identify greater numbers of targets faster, and at greater distances, to counter and defeat increasingly sophisticated threats.

The APG-83 radar can used for the suppression or destruction of enemy air defences, to include targeting radars and surface-air-missiles.

DOT&E: AN OFFICIAL OVERVIEW

In its 2021 annual report, the DOT&E stated that the APG-83 full-rate production decision, scheduled for March 2023, was currently at risk due to insufficient coordination and funding by the US Air Force for the various hardware upgrades required to modernise F-16 aircraft.

At the time, the *DOT&E 2021 Annual Report* was published in January 2021, the US Air National Guard had already acquired and was fielding 72 APG-83 radars with an initial capability to meet a US Northern Command Joint Emergent Operational Need (JEON) for homeland defence.

This initial JEON fielding was not under the oversight of the DOT&E but included Phase 1 and Phase 2 developmental and operational testing of some APG-83 capabilities and reliability enhancements. The JEON programme was originally planned for completion in July 2021, but was delayed due to production issues.

Based on the JEON Phase 1 and Phase 2, the US Air Force approved the F-16 RMP to enter at Phase 3 and Milestone C in March 2021. Milestone C is a review of a defence programme led by a Milestone Decision Authority (a team) at the end of the Engineering and Manufacturing Development phase of the defence acquisition process. Its purpose is to make a recommendation or seek approval to enter the programme into the production phase.

In Phase 1, the US Air National Guard tested, fielded, and acquired 24 radars to meet a US Northern Command Joint Emergent Operational Need Statement (JEONS) for homeland defence. Phase 1 was completed in FY2020.

In the follow-on Phase 2, the US Air National Guard acquired 48 additional APG-83 radars. Phase 2 was completed in FY2022.

Phase 3, which is on DOT&E oversight, intends to deliver full APG-83 capability and the purchase of up to 450 radars for F-16 aircraft operated by the active-duty and the Air Force Reserve. In January, the RMP Program Office was planning to make a full-rate production decision in mid-FY2023.

Because the US Air Force had not submitted a test plan for approval, the DOT&E was unable to assess the adequacy of test activities of the APG-83 radar. Only working-level discussions between the RMP Program Office, the Operational Test Agency, and DOT&E had taken place at the time the 2021 report was published. The DOT&E said: "The US Air Force has not adequately resourced the programme nor submitted a TEMP for approval that includes an IOT&E and FOT&E plan with resources to support operational testing. There is very high risk to the F-16 RMP full-rate production timeline based on this failure to develop and resource an adequate IOT&E plan."

IOT&E and FOT&E refer to initial operational test and evaluation and follow-on operational test and evaluation.

Consequently, assessments of the APG-83's operational effectiveness, its operational suitability, and its survivability in a cyber-contested environment were pending approval of an adequate test plan, completion of IOT&E, and analysis of operational testing results.

One year later, the *DOT&E 2022 Annual Report* said that a test plan had still not been formally submitted to DOT&E for approval and noted that the US Air Force was conducting final coordination on the draft test plan for planned submission in November 2022.

In its 2022 annual report, the DOT&E said the APG-83's IOT&E was being conducted in accordance with a DOT&E approved test plan, and with its oversight. Testing was said to be adequate to assess the radar capabilities being delivered at the time and that inconsistent programme funding and unexpected engineering challenges had delayed other components of the F-16 weapons system, which had prevented full realisation of APG-83 capability.

The RMP Program Office had directed a cooperative vulnerability investigation of the

Maintainers from the 96th Test Wing prepare an F-16C for a test flight at Eglin Air Force Base, Florida, July 2, 2020. The mission assessed the APG-83 radar's functionality between four aircraft all equipped with the Northrop Grumman sensor. US Air Force/MSgt Tristan McIntire

APG-83 radar installed in an F-16 aircraft assigned to the 40th Flight Test Squadron based at Eglin Air Force Base, Florida in April 2022. Some parts of the required testing that could not be tested on an F-16 aircraft at Eglin were scheduled to be completed in laboratories by the 309th Software Engineering Group at Hill Air Force Base, Utah, in February 2023. An adversarial assessment was also planned to finish up the APG-83's IOT&E.

In January 2022, the DOT&E reported that operational testing of the APG-83 conducted by that date provided compelling evidence that the APG-83 is a significant improvement over the legacy APG-68. That judgement despite the absence of some of the APG-83's required capabilities. At the time, the APG-83 performance was limited by the F-16's aging mission computers, obsolete data system, and insufficient network architecture. The upgrades of these sub-systems were either delayed or had failed to meet mission requirements. According to the DOT&E, the most significant upgrade is the transition from MIL-STD-1553 data buses to Ethernet, which is part of the high-speed data network project.

In terms of suitability, the *DOT&E 2022 Annual Report* said: "Early data suggests that the APG-83 will be suitable. Although the US Air Force has identified some maintenance challenges due to tight clearances between the radome and air data system, the radar has shown vast improvements in overall maintainability over the legacy APG-68. Pilots are generally satisfied with the human-systems interface, although some limitations and trade-offs were required to integrate it with existing F-16 systems. The trade-offs result in increased pilot workload for some tasks, such as switching between different displays based on radar mode and function in use."

In the same annual report, the DOT&E said the APG-83's survivability in a

APG-83 SCALABLE AGILE BEAM RADAR TIMELINE

Date	Activity	Notes
November 2009	An APG-83 trial unit was test-flown on an F-16 at Edwards Air Force Base, California.	
December 14, 2014	Northrop Grumman delivered the first engineering, manufacturing, and development APG-83 radar unit to Lockheed Martin.	The APG-83 was competitively selected by Lockheed Martin for the F-16 Radar Modernization Program (RMP) to support US Air Force and Taiwan Air Force F-16 upgrade programmes.
February 3, 2015	Northrop Grumman engineers began work on the first production series APG-83 radar after the first production order from Lockheed Martin.	Under the Lockheed Martin order, Northrop Grumman delivered 142 radars to Lockheed Martin for the Taiwan Air Force F-16 upgrade programme.
End of 2016	Northrop Grumman delivered the first production APG-83 radar sets for Taiwan, its first international customer.	Production of export APG-83 SABR radars started in 2016 and Northrop Grumman began delivering production APG-83 radars for its first international customer on schedule at the end of 2016.
2017	First US Air National Guard contract award for 72 APG-83 radars followed by a second contract for 15 EMD and 90 production radars for the US Air Force.	If all contract options are exercised, up to 372 radars could be procured by 2027.
As of March 23, 2017	The US Air Force F-16 developmental test squadron, the 416th Flight Test Squadron based at Edwards Air Force Base, California, had completed several ground and flight tests since 2015. Data collected was used to determine the radar's operational suitability.	
June 7, 2017	The US Air Force selected the APG-83 for its F-16 RMP, this a different selection to the one made by the US Air National Guard.	
January 2020	The US Air National Guard started fielding the APG-83 radar.	At the time more than 200 APG-83 radar units had been built at Northrop Grumman's radar assembly facility in Baltimore, for US and international customers.
September 21-25, 2020	The District of Columbia Air National Guard's 113th Wing employed the APG-83 during Exercise Guardian Shield 20-02.	Guardian Shield was the largest live-fly cruise missile defence exercise ever held by the Department of Defense.
By October 2020	The Operational Flight Program Combined Test Force comprising Air Materiel Command's 40th Flight Test Squadron and Air Combat Command's 85th Test and Evaluation Squadron successfully tested the APG-83 radar during a four-ship F-16 mission flown from Eglin Air Force Base, Florida.	The mission was the first of its kind to assess the APG-83 radar on four fighter aircraft at the same time. Multi-ship missions enable the test teams to evaluate the behaviour of the APG-83 radar with four aircraft in close-proximity, and to verify if the four radars interfere with each other, degrading the signal, or if they work better, improving the signal.
By October 2020	The District of Columbia, South Carolina ANG and an unspecified base had completed their respective APG-83 radar upgrade and South Dakota was underway.	
October 15, 2020	The US Air National Guard met full operational capability readiness for the APG-83 radar on its F-16s.	
July 14, 2021	Northrop Grumman Corporation announced it had adopted lean-agile methodologies in the development and integration of the APG-83 radar software. The methods enabled software updates to be delivered and tested on the F-16 in weeks instead of the months taken using the traditional waterfall method.	Software development was conducted in partnership with teams based at Hill and Eglin Air Force Bases, and the Air National Guard Air Force Reserve Command Test Center at Tucson.
September 09, 2021	Northrop Grumman's Next Generation Electronic Warfare (NGEW) system and APG-83 radar made the first combined test flight on the company's testbed CRJ during Exercise Northern Lightning. During the exercise, the NGEW flew 170 test points against ground-based threat emitters. NGEW is not in production for the US Air Force but was granted authority to develop the system using existing technology.	
Northrop Grumman expected to begin NGEW developmental test on F-16s during Q1 FY2022.	NGEW and the APG-83 demonstrated full pulse-to-pulse, multi-function interoperability in a contested operational environment. The APG-83 successfully engaged multiple air and ground targets, NGEW detected and identified a range of advanced threats, and employed advanced jamming techniques capable of defeating those threats when required.	
January 20, 2023	Northrop Grumman Mission Systems was scheduled to begin full rate production of the latest APG-83 radar in 2023.	

F-16 Falcon Still in the Fight

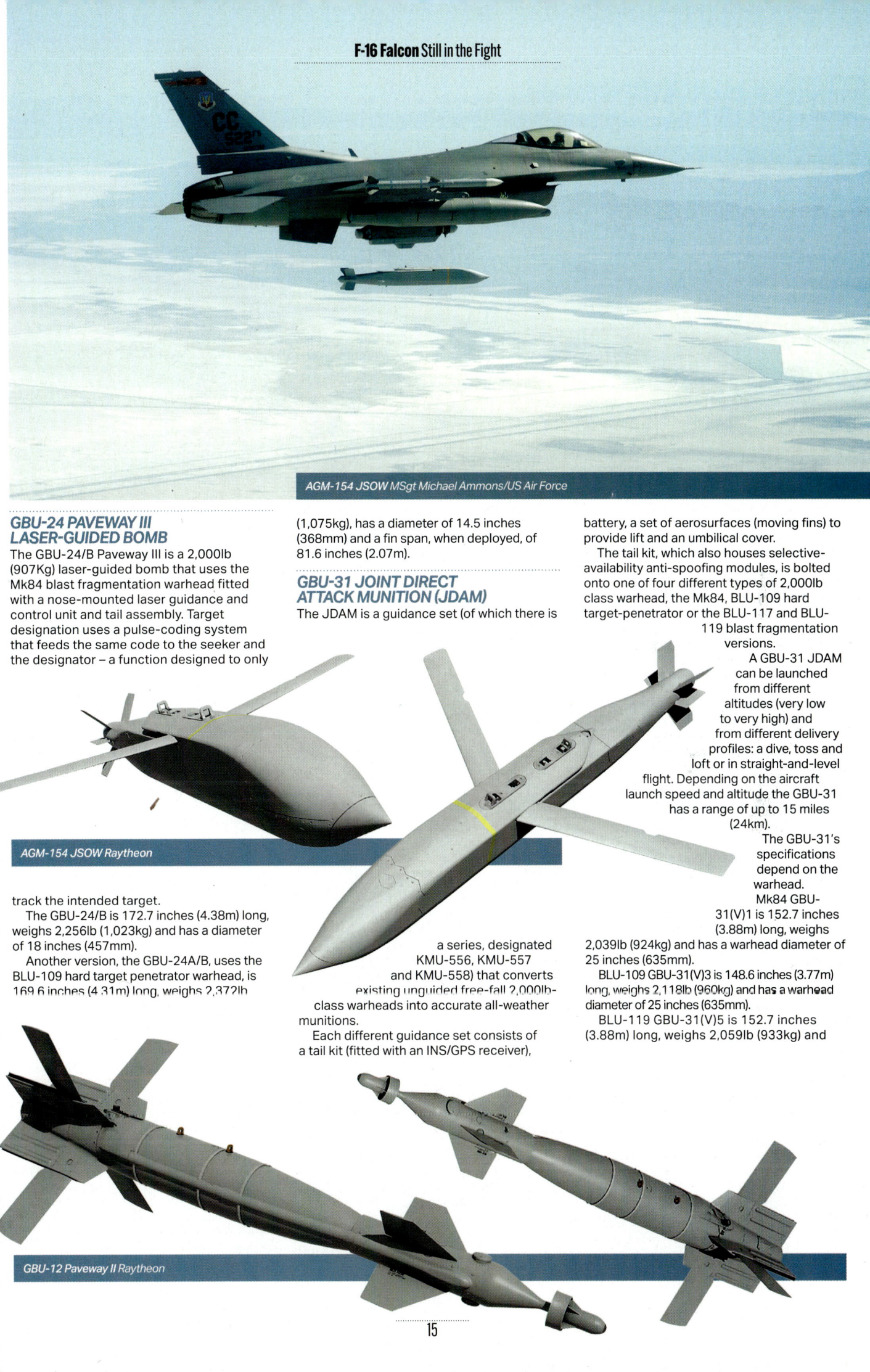

AGM-154 JSOW MSgt Michael Ammons/US Air Force

AGM-154 JSOW Raytheon

GBU-12 Paveway II Raytheon

GBU-24 PAVEWAY III LASER-GUIDED BOMB

The GBU-24/B Paveway III is a 2,000lb (907Kg) laser-guided bomb that uses the Mk84 blast fragmentation warhead fitted with a nose-mounted laser guidance and control unit and tail assembly. Target designation uses a pulse-coding system that feeds the same code to the seeker and the designator – a function designed to only track the intended target.

The GBU-24/B is 172.7 inches (4.38m) long, weighs 2,256lb (1,023kg) and has a diameter of 18 inches (457mm).

Another version, the GBU-24A/B, uses the BLU-109 hard target penetrator warhead, is 169.6 inches (4.31m) long, weighs 2,372lb (1,075kg), has a diameter of 14.5 inches (368mm) and a fin span, when deployed, of 81.6 inches (2.07m).

GBU-31 JOINT DIRECT ATTACK MUNITION (JDAM)

The JDAM is a guidance set (of which there is a series, designated KMU-556, KMU-557 and KMU-558) that converts existing unguided free-fall 2,000lb-class warheads into accurate all-weather munitions.

Each different guidance set consists of a tail kit (fitted with an INS/GPS receiver), battery, a set of aerosurfaces (moving fins) to provide lift and an umbilical cover.

The tail kit, which also houses selective-availability anti-spoofing modules, is bolted onto one of four different types of 2,000lb class warhead, the Mk84, BLU-109 hard target-penetrator or the BLU-117 and BLU-119 blast fragmentation versions.

A GBU-31 JDAM can be launched from different altitudes (very low to very high) and from different delivery profiles: a dive, toss and loft or in straight-and-level flight. Depending on the aircraft launch speed and altitude the GBU-31 has a range of up to 15 miles (24km).

The GBU-31's specifications depend on the warhead.

Mk84 GBU-31(V)1 is 152.7 inches (3.88m) long, weighs 2,039lb (924kg) and has a warhead diameter of 25 inches (635mm).

BLU-109 GBU-31(V)3 is 148.6 inches (3.77m) long, weighs 2,118lb (960kg) and has a warhead diameter of 25 inches (635mm).

BLU-119 GBU-31(V)5 is 152.7 inches (3.88m) long, weighs 2,059lb (933kg) and has a warhead diameter of 25 inches (635mm).

GBU-38 JOINT DIRECT ATTACK MUNITION (JDAM)

The GBU-38 uses a KMU-572 guidance set to convert existing unguided free-fall 500lb-class bombs into accurate all-weather munitions.

The tail kit, which also houses selective availability anti-spoofing modules, is bolted onto either the Mk82 or BLU-126 500lb class warhead.

The GBU-38's specifications depend on the warhead.

Mk82 GBU-38(V)1 is 95.2 inches (2.41m) long, weighs 552lb (250kg) and has a warhead diameter of 17 inches (431mm).

The only difference of the BLU-126 GBU-31(V)4 version is a slightly higher weight to the (V)1 of 558lb (253kg).

GBU-39/B SMALL DIAMETER BOMB (SDB)

The GBU-39/B is a 250lb-class autonomous conventional air-to-ground precision glide weapon designed for striking fixed and stationary re-locatable targets from stand-off range. It consists of the weapon and the BRU-61/A four-place miniature munition pneumatic carriage system.

An advanced anti-jam GPS-aided INS provides guidance to the co-ordinates of a stationary target.

SDB has a multi-purpose penetrating/blast fragmentation warhead coupled with a cockpit-selectable electronic fuse.

ADM-160C MALD Raytheon

A proximity sensor provides a height of burst capability.

After launch the SDB's wings deploy and it glides to the target using GPS guidance up to a range of more than 60 miles (96km).

The GBU-39 measures 70.8 inches (1.80m) long, 7.5 inches (190mm) wide, has a wingspan of 152.4 inches (3.87m) and weighs 285lb (129kg).

GBU-38 JDAM Capt Shannon Miles/US Air Force

GBU-54 LASER JOINT DIRECT ATTACK MUNITION (LJDAM)

The GBU-54 LJDAM is a GPS/INS guided, autonomous, all-weather attack weapon for use against fixed and moving targets.

The 500lb class munition comprises a GBU-38 JDAM fitted with a Precision Laser Guidance Set (PLGS) that gives optional semi-active laser guidance. The PLGS is a passive laser seeker that can be easily installed in the field to the front of existing GBU-38 JDAM weapons and is connected to the guidance set via an externally mounted strap-on harness kit. The GBU-54 LJDAM was developed as an urgent operational need, and testing was completed in less than 17 months. It was first delivered in May 2008 and deployed in combat in Iraq three months later.

Built from a Mk82 warhead, the GBU-54 is 95.2 inches (2.41m) long, weighs 552lb (250kg), has a warhead diameter of 17 inches (431mm), and a range of up to 15 miles (24km).

ADM-160C MINIATURE AIR-LAUNCHED DECOY-JAMMER (MALD-J)

The MALD-J is an air-launched, expendable decoy/jammer designed to deceive, saturate and jam an enemy integrated air defence system, but is technically a missile. It is classed as a stand-in jammer and requires much less power than the stand-off systems integrated on the EA-18G Growler. Its low power requirement is sufficient for the jamming role because the missile can operate much closer to a target.

The ADM-160C comprises a forward payload section housing the electronic warfare elements and a larger aft section, called the truck, which houses the GPS-aided INS or GAINS navigation system.

Its pre-programmed flight path is controlled by rear-mounted actuator control fins and variable sweep wings that translate to keep the centre of gravity in the right position from the centre of pressure, and sweep back and forth to control airspeed.

The MALD-J is powered by a Pratt & Whitney TJ-150 turbojet engine, uses JP-10 propellant, has a dedicated mission range of 500 nautical miles (925km) depending on the air speed and altitude chosen for the profile or 50 minutes loiter after a 200 nautical mile (370km) dash.

As the missile releases from the pylon a lanyard pulls to switch the battery on, initiates a search for satellites, invokes self-orientation and starts the engine.

Northrop Grumman's CRJ flight test bed fitted with an F-16 nose radome housing an APG-83 radar unit. Northrop Grumman

APG-83 CAPABILITIES

The APG-83 AESA provides the following capabilities.
- Autonomous, all-environment stand-off precision targeting.
- Large area, high-definition, synthetic aperture radar capability called Big SAR. This mode provides pilots with unprecedented target area detail and digital map displays that can be tailored with slew and zoom features, which enables greater situational awareness, flexibility, and quicker all-weather targeting.
- Advanced processing and proprietary algorithms automatically scan entire SAR maps, precisely locate, and classify targets of interest, and greatly reduce pilot workload.
- High quality, coordinate generation.
- Electronically scanned beams enable faster area searches, resulting in earlier and longer-range target acquisition and tracking.
- Smaller target detection.
- Multi-target tracking.
- Approximately 95% of the APG-83's operating modes come directly from the APG-81 radar, including robust and proven electronic protection to counter advanced threats.
- Enhanced combat ID.
- Electronic scanning ensures rapid target updates and makes interleaved mode operations possible for greater mission effectiveness, situational awareness, and survivability.

Maritime modes.
- A single line replaceable unit containing the receiver, exciter, and processor functions.
- Three to five times greater reliability and availability.

cyber-contested environment could not yet be assessed. Data from the cooperative vulnerability investigation and upcoming adversarial assessment would provide insights into the new radar's capabilities and limitations in a cyber-contested environment. The cooperative vulnerability investigation did provide useful system stability information independent of threat cyber effects.

APG-83: THE STORY SO FAR

In a series of questions about the APG-83 radar submitted to Northrop Grumman, Mark Rossi, director, SABR programmes said: "Northrop Grumman has been the sole radar provider for the F-16 for over four decades. The company has a history of keeping the F-16 relevant through technology upgrades of our mechanically scanned APG-66 and APG-68 radars. The APG-83 upgrade is a drop-in replacement of previous radars and moves this platform from the limitations of mechanically scanned radars to the simultaneous, multifunction capability of an AESA radar. The greater bandwidth, speed and agility of the APG-83 enables the F-16 to detect, track and identify a greater number of targets faster and at longer ranges, whether in the air or on the ground.

Four APG-83-equipped F-16Cs await take-off clearance for the four-ship mission flown by pilots assigned to the Operational Flight Program Combined Test Force on July 2, 2020. US Air Force/MSgt Tristan McIntire

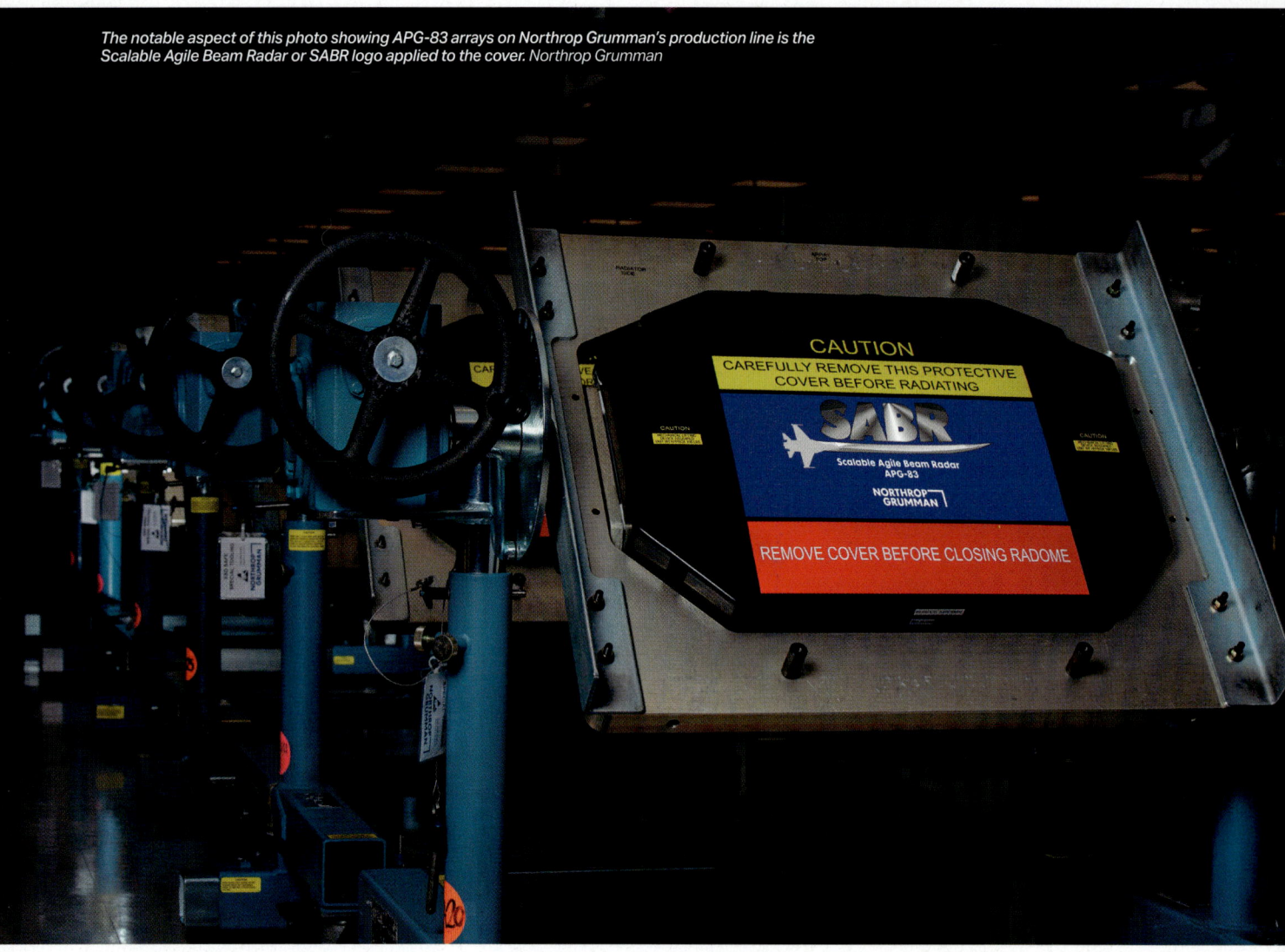

The notable aspect of this photo showing APG-83 arrays on Northrop Grumman's production line is the Scalable Agile Beam Radar or SABR logo applied to the cover. Northrop Grumman

"Northrop Grumman's APG-83 Scalable Agile Beam Radar (SABR) was developed for the F-16. Prior to its production, Northrop Grumman developed the mechanically scanned (M-scan) APG-68 radar system for the F-16. The APG-68's M-scan array enabled protection from air-to-air and air-to-surface threats with greater accuracy compared to other legacy F-16 fire control radars. M-scan radars had to be physically moved to steer the radar beam and were limited to a single operating mode at any one time. Either air-to-air or air-to-ground but not both simultaneously. Due to limitations of certain frequencies, the APG-68 was also unable to detect and track multiple threats at a time.

"The APG-83 AESA is a powerful upgrade to the previous M-scan, capable of operating in multiple modes including one for maritime search. It enables the F-16 to detect, track and identify a greater number of targets faster and at longer ranges than ever before."

In a US Air Force press release issued on July 2, 2020, following the first mission flown by four F-16Cs each fitted with an APG-83 radar, Jack Harman, an F-16 test pilot assigned to the Eglin-based 40th Flight Test Squadron said: "The APG-83's capability allows us to target the northwest corner of a small building or the cockpit of an aircraft from several miles away, beyond line-of-sight. The APG-83 improves our ability to identify the threat prior to us being targeted – we no longer must be inside a threat envelope to detect it."

By testing four APG-83 radars at the same time, the Operational Flight Program Combined Test Force, comprising the 40th Flight Test Squadron and the 85th Test and Evaluation Squadron, was able to assess whether the aircraft experienced interference and evaluated if the signal improved or degraded while operating together. The four-ship is the basic fighting formation of fighter aircraft, and allowed the testers to see how the radar responds in a combat scenario.

Detailing the APG-83's compatibility with the APG-81, Marc Rossi said: "The APG-83 system is over 90% compatible to Northrop Grumman's APG-81 AESA radar which equips all F-35 Lightning II stealth fighters and uses the electronic protection capabilities of the APG-81."

As an insight to the functionality of the APG-83 radar it's worth taking a quick look at the APG-81. In terms of type, the APG-81 is a pulse-Doppler radar system that runs multiple waveforms for air-to-air and air-to-ground. The front end of the radar comprises the array, the T/R modules, and the radiating element. The front end is bolted directly to the integrated forebody and positioned up front in the radome.

The APG-81 has an electronically steered array controlled by a steering computer with no mechanical motion. Designed as a multi-mode system, the APG-81 has 32 modes of operation: 12 air-to-air, 12 air-to-ground (including two maritime modes: ship target track and sea search), four electronic warfare (electronic attack and electronic protection), two navigation, and two weather. Some of the modes are high resolution and are supported by the sophisticated signal processing available.

TESTING THE APG-83

Explaining the consecutive test phases of the APG-83, Rossi said: "There has been a series of testing procedures for the APG-83 that vary depending on the development stage of the radar. When first developed the APG-83 went through a series of development lab testing from integration to quality. As the APG-83 was developed, the radar system went through extensive flight testing on the company's CRJ aircraft. By using the CRJ, Northrop Grumman was able to replicate the installation conditions of the F-16 for the purposes of testing. The CRJ's standard nose was removed, the APG-83 radar was configured onto the front of the aircraft and then a replica of an F-16 nose was installed on the CRJ. This allows for us to test and collect data from the radar that should mimic what an F-16 pilot will see.

"Each radar system is also tested for operational functionality and then flight tested each time there is a software update. The

APG-83 is software defined and hardware enabled, which speeds up development time and eliminates reconfiguring hardware for every upgrade, and customer changes and upgrades can be completed through software integration only."

Describing the integration effort for the APG-83 on an F-16 fighter, Marc Rossi described the APG-83 as a drop in replacement radar for Northrop Grumman's mechanically scanned radar: "We were able to use our flight proven knowledge and understanding of the F-16 to create the APG-83. Installation was simple as the radar was intended to fit perfectly with the F-16's current design in terms of both electronic and physical connections.

"For example, the APG-83 has its own liquid cooling system that is completely self-contained to the radar. Think of it as a more advanced version of a car radiator. The coolant is chilled by an existing system on the aircraft, so no additional modifications were needed to fit an APG-83 to an F-16."

Northrop Grumman flew an APG-83 radar installed on an F-16 for the first time in 2009.

Because of the company's prior knowledge of the aircraft, Northrop Grumman can retrofit the APG-83 in less than a week. The new F-16 radar is being installed at military bases throughout the United States and around the world. Many are installed in country by local representatives and contractors to meet the specific needs of that customer.

This image provides an idea of the APG-83 array; the hundreds of T/R modules are hidden by a cover. Northrop Grumman

Northrop Grumman test mechanics manhandle an F-16 nose radome for fitting to the company's CRJ flight test bed. Northrop Grumman

F-16 Falcon Still in the Fight

Have Glass: Making the F-16 Less Detectable

Jon Lake provides an overview of a programme dubbed Have Glass which seeks to make an F-16 fighter less detectable to radar.

Today's fifth-generation types incorporate a degree of low observability that gives them a much-reduced RCS compared to conventional aircraft. But the low RCS is a function of optimised design, purpose-built structure, and advanced specialised materials. Radar cross section can be measured in dBm² (decibels per square metre) or more simply in square metres. However, in the latter case, the radar cross section of an aircraft is different from its actual cross-sectional area.

Instead, the RCS is quoted in terms of the equivalent area of a metal sphere that would reflect back the same radar energy as the aircraft, when viewed at the same altitude, from straight ahead. For example, the Lockheed Martin F-22 Raptor reportedly has a frontal RCS of 0.0001-0.0002m², equivalent to a marble-sized sphere, while the F-35A reportedly has an RCS of about 0.0015m² – equivalent to a golf ball-sized metal sphere.

This kind of RCS makes an immediate tactical difference – an F-22 can be detected by an APG-68 or and an APG-80 fighter radar, but only at ranges of 5-10km, far too late for defensive systems to react.

Of course, the LO fifth-generation fighters are designed for something close to 'all aspect' stealth – having a low radar cross section when viewed from any angle.

This is difficult to achieve, and some aircraft that are thought of as being LO aircraft are not

Three F-16s from Eglin Air Force Base prepare for take-off. This shot shows two things. One, the difference between an F-16 painted in traditional grey (furthest from camera) and the dark textured Have Glass paint. Two, the Have Glass paint appears of a different shade based on how sunlight strikes the aircraft's fuselage.
US Air Force/MSgt Tristan McIntire

F-16 Falcon Still in the Fight

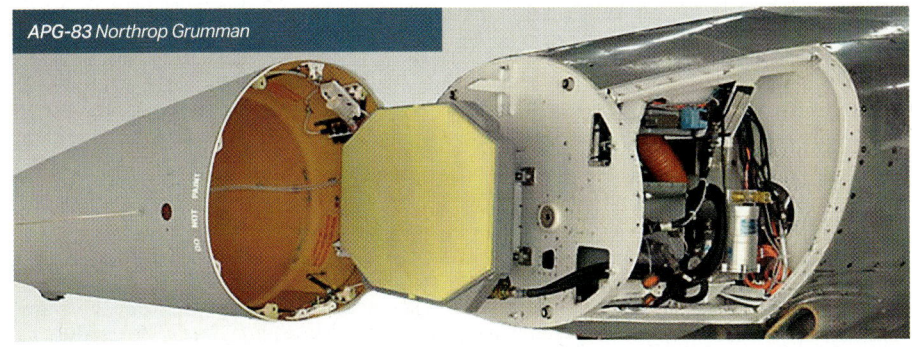

APG-83 Northrop Grumman

and target acquisition using interleaved modes. An MSA is limited to one mode at a time.

The SABR attracted Taiwanese investment (reportedly $300 million for development which represented one third of total CAPES development funding) and from other potential FMS partners, looking for a near-term upgrade capability.

A prototype of a SABR radar unit fitted in Northrop Grumman's BAC-111 test bed, demonstrated electronic protection (EP) capabilities against a range of simulated electronic attack (EA) and other threats. A second prototype was tested on a US Air Force Block 50 F-16. For a complete overview of the APG-83 radar see *APG-83 Scalable Agile Beam Radar p18-23*.

RAYTHEON APG-84 RACR

The X-band RACR was developed from Raytheon's earlier AESA radar systems: the APG-63(V)3 used by the F-15SG, the APG-79 used by the F/A-18E/F Super Hornet and the APG-82(V)1 for the F-15E Strike Eagle. A RACR unit made it maiden flight integrated on US Air Force F-16D 87-0392/'ED' at Edwards Air Force Base California on July 30, 2010.

As it reportedly features more than 90% commonality with the APG-79, the RACR design had the potential to benefit from hardware and software fixes developed to improve performance of, and from upgrades designed to enable network connectivity with the APG-79. The Super Hornet AESA radar is scheduled to remain in service until the 2040s.

Raytheon says the RACR offers higher resolution, a longer stand-off range, simultaneous detection, identification and tracking of multiple air and surface targets and up to ten times more operational availability than MSA radars, with correspondingly reduced life-cycle costs.

THE FUTURE

The US Air Force did not give up on procuring an AESA radar system for its F-16s. In 2015, the air force issued a request for information (RfI) for a Modular Mission Computer Upgrade (MMCU) suitable for 630 F-16s to be upgraded with an AESA capability.

Following this, in 2015, the US Air Force's 1st Air Force based at Tyndall Air Force Base, Florida, submitted a classified urgent operational need statement (UON), stating it needed F-16 radar upgrades to carry out its homeland defence mission. At the time, the Air National Guard, which flew 37% of the total US Air Force F-16 force and held the majority of the air sovereignty alert missions, especially wanted an AESA to engage cruise missiles and unmanned air vehicle (UAV) targets. The UON reportedly specifically requested the SABR be retrofitted to 340 of the Guard's Block 30 F-16s and asked for FY 2015 dollars to be reprogrammed to pay for them; the FY 2016 dollars requested would not be available in time.

UONs issued at the time were normally met within 180 days, although the scope of the proposed radar upgrade led to it being expanded to 24 months. Instead of the comprehensive CAPES upgrade, the US Air Force looked for a low-cost solution. To meet demanding cost and schedule needs of the programme, it was proposed the upgrade would comprise an air-to-air only AESA or a pulse Doppler air-to-ground upgrade, rather than a SABR Block 2.0. This would limit the future multi-mission capabilities of the Air National Guard's Block 30 aircraft. Major General Timothy Ray, the US Air Force's acquisition director of global power programmes at the time, told a House Armed Services Committee hearing on March 26, 2015, that if some ANG Block 30 F-16s are upgraded with an air-to-air-only AESA to meet the UON timeframe, "we will lose some capabilities over what we have now".

Acknowledging the proposed funding level was far less than would be needed to revive CAPES, the then Air Force Chief of Staff General Mark Welsh told the House Armed Services Committee on March 17, 2015: "We need to develop an AESA radar plan for our F-16s that conduct the homeland defence mission in particular." He reminded the Representatives that, "Our entire fleet – active, Guard and Reserve – none of them have been upgraded with that radar."

Rather than beginning procurement of the SABR, on March 6, 2015, the US Air Force issued an official "sources sought" to meet the UON, that would potentially consider low-cost radar solutions, intended to upgrade a wide range of fighter designs, such as the Selex Galileo ES-05 (used by the Gripen), Grifo-E or Vixen 500E/1000 and Israel's Elta EL/M-2052. The Israeli radar could not be used to upgrade Israeli F-16s because of US export control restrictions governing source code release.

The US Air Force then focussed on re-equipping a single squadron to meet the UON. The 113th Fighter Wing of the District of Columbia Air National Guard based at Andrews Air Force Base, Maryland, was selected as the first unit to get its F-16s upgraded. The air force said all 24 aircraft assigned to the 113th FW would be upgraded with the SABR, starting in 2015, paid for with $113 million reprogrammed from the FY 2015 budget and be completed by mid-2017.

The process for upgrading F-16 radars seemed uncertain to the Senate Appropriations Committee, which supported a broader upgrade than just 24 F-16s. Unsure of where the air force was heading, the committee put language in the FY 2016 defence appropriations bill requiring a report to Congress on planned F-16 upgrades.

AAQ-13 AND AAQ-14 LANTIRN PODS

The Lockheed Martin (originally Martin Marietta) LANTIRN (Low-Altitude Navigation and Targeting Infrared for Night) system was originally developed in the 1980s. It was the first and most widely produced targeting and navigation pod used by the F-16, and 1,400 entered service with ten countries.

LANTIRN provides an all-weather capability for weapons delivery. It is a unique system that provides terrain-following capability for high-speed, low-altitude all-weather operations.

LANTIRN is a twin-pod system, combining the AAQ-13 navigation pod and AAQ-14 targeting pod. It was introduced into US Air Force service in 1987 and equipped some US Air Force F-16s during Operation

APG-84 Raytheon

APG-84 Raytheon

Desert Storm in 1991, its first major combat use. Since then it was widely used and integrated with multiple aircraft types.

The AAQ-13 navigation pod provides high-speed, low-altitude precision attack capability with a wide field-of-view FLIR (forward-looking infrared) sensor and Raytheon's Ku-band terrain-following radar (TFR). The two sensors provide a picture displayed on the pilot's head-up display (HUD) and adequate night vision for safe low-level flying.

The AAQ-13 is linked to the aircraft's control system in terrain-following mode to ensure it stays at a preset altitude above the ground. The TFR capability was not available in some export versions – designated AAQ-20 Pathfinder.

The AAQ-14 targeting pod contains a stabilised wide and narrow field-of-view FLIR sensor for day/night target acquisition and targeting of precision-guided weapons with a laser designator and rangefinder. The pod is designed with a maximum operating altitude of 25,000ft (7,620m).

The pilot uses the AAQ-14 to detect a target with the FLIR's wide field-of-view function cued by the radar or widely used precision, day/night navigation and targeting pod.

It won the US Precision Attack Targeting System competition in 1998 and 168 pods were ordered for Air National Guard and Air Force Reserve Command F-16s. The system was fielded in 1999 as the AN/AAQ-28(V)1, the first in a series adopted by the US military.

Northrop Grumman, the licence holder for US production, upgraded the system to (V)2 standard by incorporating an improved FLIR, laser target marker and updated software.

The AAQ-28(V)3 LITENING ER (Extended Range) version, fielded in 2001, included a FLIR with increased range and greater resolution. The AAQ-28(V)6 LITENING AT (Advanced Technology) version, fielded in 2003, provided even greater range, accurate target co-ordinate generation and multi-target cueing.

The LITENING G4 (Generation Four) was first delivered to the US Air Force in 2008. It features an improved mid-wave FLIR, a new laser illuminator, two CCD TV sensors (one with

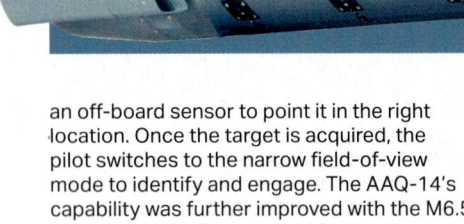

AAQ-28 LITENING Northrop Grumman

wide and one with narrow field-of-view), laser spot tracker and an infrared laser marker. It has improved target recognition capabilities resulting from the incorporation of the laser target-imaging programme, including short-wave infra red laser-augmented imaging. This enhances the ability to capture images in conditions where the medium-wave infrared FLIR and CCD are less effective. The first international deliveries were to Denmark.

The AAQ-28(V)7 and (V)9 LITENING SE (Sensor Enhancement) versions, featuring a two-way digital data link, were ordered by the US Air Force as one of the two winning designs in a 2010 competition. In 2014, the air force started to upgrade its (V)1 and (V)2 versions to (V)7 standard.

The Rafael-produced LITENING G4 Advanced with an air-to-air capability (offered as the G5 to the US) was announced in early 2015.

F-16 operators: Chile, Denmark, Indonesia, Israel, the Netherlands, Portugal, Singapore, the US Air Force, the Air National Guard, and Venezuela used the LITENING system.

AAQ-33 SNIPER POD

The Lockheed Martin Sniper Advanced Targeting Pod was first ordered by the US Air Force in 2001. The single-pod system was integrated on the F-16 with the M4 OFP software installed between 2005 (the year Sniper entered operational service) and 2007.

The pod features a third-generation, mid-wavelength FLIR, a high-definition dual field-of-view CCD TV and a laser target designator, spot tracker and rangefinder and, perhaps most significantly, a two-way Link 16-compatible data link which feeds imagery and streaming video to other aircraft or ground units. This data link capability entered US Air Force service with the M4.2 OFP in 2007.

an off-board sensor to point it in the right location. Once the target is acquired, the pilot switches to the narrow field-of-view mode to identify and engage. The AAQ-14's capability was further improved with the M6.5 Operational Flight Program (OFP) software installed on F-16 MLU (Mid-Life Update) aircraft starting in 2014.

The AAQ-19 Pathfinder version was exported without the capability to designate AGM-65 Maverick air-to-surface missiles and lacks some air-to-air operating modes.

AAQ-19 AND AAQ-20 LANTIRN-ER PODS

The upgraded LANTIRN-ER (Extended Range) system was introduced in the late 1990s. It is fitted to US Air Force and international F-16s and features a charge-coupled device (CCD) TV camera, a laser rangefinder/designator effective up to 40,000ft (12,192m) and a laser spot tracker.

Other components have been incorporated in LANTIRN pods, including the Northrop Grumman laser designator ranger.

F-16 operators: Belgium, Denmark, Egypt (unconfirmed), Greece, Israel (unconfirmed), Republic of Korea (unconfirmed), the Netherlands, the US Air Force, US Air Force Reserve Command and the Air National Guard used the LANTIRN-ER system.

AAQ-28(V) LITENING POD

The original LITENING pod, designed by Israel's Rafael in the early 1990s, was the most

AAQ-33 SNIPER-SE POD

An improved version called Sniper-SE (Sensor Enhancement) was approved for procurement by the US Air Force in 2010. The air force subsequently decided to split any future pod order between the Sniper-SE (60%) and the Northrop Grumman LITENING SE (40%).

One hundred Sniper SE pods were delivered to the US Air Force between 2010 and 2014. Despite a requirement for a further 1,100, the US Air Force halted pod procurement because of a shortage of money.

On March 27, 2015, Lockheed Martin was awarded a sole-source indefinite-delivery/indefinite-quantity contract to provide multiple Sniper-SE targeting pods to the US Air Force.

The Sniper-SE's improved laser guidance algorithms enable engagement of moving targets, including ships. Its two-way data link can share video, co-ordinates and imagery (annotated or otherwise) with a Joint Terminal Attack Controller (JTAC) who has a Link 16-compatible ROVER (Remote Operated Video Enhanced Receiver) terminal. The pilot is able to receive and view imagery annotated with target details and co-ordinates from the JTAC.

F-16 users: Egypt, Iraq, Jordan, Romania (planned), Portugal (unconfirmed), Thailand, the US Air Force and the Air National Guard.

DB-110 RECONNAISSANCE SYSTEM

The DB-110 is a digital, real-time, tactical reconnaissance system that captures extremely high-quality images day and night using electro-optical/infrared (EO/IR) technology, all contained within in a single sensor gimbal. The system incorporates a dual-band day and night time imaging sensor, a real-time digital recorder and a real-time data transmission capability within a single pod.

Once airborne, mounted on either a manned or unmanned platform, the DB-110 system provides proven tactical imaging capability over long, medium, and short stand-off ranges, including over-flight imaging.

AAQ-33 SNIPER Lockheed Martin

Pre-planned points of interest can be imaged and the data transmitted in real time to analysts on the ground, as well as viewed inside the cockpit of an F-16 fighter (for example on its multi-function display, MFD). This enables the pilot to exploit each target in real time and verify targets and then re-task the system to capture images revealed on an 'opportunity basis' during the

Above: AIM-120C AMRAAM   Opposite: AGM-65D Maverick TSgt Michael Ammons/US Air Force

The most valuable – and costly – element of upgrades to F-16 fighters is an active electronically scanned array (AESA) radar. Today, more than 2,300 of the original Northrop Grumman APG-66 and APG-68 radars in F-16s worldwide are candidates for upgrading. An AESA retrofit increases F-16 capability across multiple mission areas, especially air-to-air against low radar cross-section targets such as stealth aircraft, cruise missiles and unmanned air vehicles.

A number of designs competed for contracts, most notably the Northrop Grumman APG-83 SABR (Scalable Agile Beam Radar) and the Raytheon APG-84 RACR (Raytheon Advanced Combat Radar). Both were designed to fit the F-16 without modification, and operate with the aircraft's current power and cooling systems. The only operational F-16 AESA is Northrop Grumman's APG-80 used on the United Arab Emirates (UAE) Block 60 F-16E and F-16Fs. This highly capable radar was the first AESA to be used in combat over Libya in 2011, but is not designed for retrofit to earlier F-16 models.

In 2013, the SABR Block 1.0 was selected for the upgrade of Taiwan's Block 20 F-16A/F-16B fleet and the Block 2.0 version for US Air Force F-16Cs and F-16Ds. It was seen as a likely system for future US Foreign Military Sale (FMS) programmes and assured commonality with the Combat Avionics Programmed Extension Suite (CAPES): an upgrade destined for 350 US Air Force F-16C and F-16D aircraft modified under a $1.8 billion programme.

The CAPES included the APG-83 SABR, an upgraded electronic warfare suite (including a new passive warning system), a new mission computer, a large cockpit centre display unit and a integrated broadcast service to allow data from off-board sensors to be data linked to the cockpit. Lockheed Martin developed a parallel airframe upgrade programme to increase structural life from 8,000 to 10,000 hours.

The CAPES upgrade aircraft initial operational capability was planned for 2020.

As prime contractor and project integrator of the CAPES programme, Lockheed Martin had been authorised by the US Air Force to select between the SABR and RACR for the Taiwan and CAPES upgrades. This gave Lockheed Martin's upgrade package a competitive advantage. Other upgrade packages were developed by Boeing (incorporating one of several types of radar and a new Boeing-developed mission computer) and BAE Systems (which incorporated the RACR). The Republic of Korea (RoK) selected the latter option. Its Defence Acquisition Program Administration (DAPA) selected the RACR for the RoKAF's 136-aircraft F-16C/F-16D fleet. Modification was to be carried out by BAE Systems and deliveries were to start in late 2016.

When the US Air Force cancelled CAPES in March 2014 (except for the cockpit display element) due to sequestration (it's funding was cut and priority was given to production of the F-35A Lightning II over upgrades), the RoKAF cancelled its order in November. The US Government also raised the price of the FMS sale by 45% to $760 million after the first two prototypes had been completed by BAE Systems at its facility in Fort Worth, Texas.

The two blows did not end Taiwan's requirement for an F-16 upgrade. The $1.85 billion upgrade programme was awarded to Lockheed Martin (as the prime contractor with the work carried out by AIDC in Taiwan) in October 2012. Nor has the worldwide need for an F-16 AESA radar diminished, see *The Viper Upgrade p32-37*.

NORTHROP GRUMMAN APG-66 AND APG-68 SERIES

The first F-16A and F-16B models were equipped with the Westinghouse (now Northrop Grumman) APG-66 X-band radar. Using a slotted planar mechanically scanned array (MSA), it had four air-to-air and seven air-to-surface operating modes. The APG-66(V)2, fitted on Block 15 aircraft, introduced a more powerful signal processor, higher power output, improved reliability and increased range in cluttered or jamming conditions. The Mid-Life Update (MLU) programme introduced the upgraded APG-66(V)2A. Early versions remaining in service include the APG-66(V)3 on Block 20s.

F-16s are currently fitted with the Northrop Grumman APG-68(V)-series (an evolution of the APG-66) with pulse Doppler range and angle track, and a multimode MSA. Compared with the APG-66, the APG-68 has improved range, higher resolution, and 25 operating modes. These include air-to-air modes for range-while-search, look-up search, velocity search with ranging, air combat, track-while-scan (up to ten targets), raid cluster resolution, single target track and pulse Doppler track to provide continuous-wave target illumination (for Raytheon AIM-7 Sparrow missiles). Air-to-surface modes include ground-mapping, Doppler beam-sharpening, ground moving target, sea target, fixed-target track, target freeze after pop-up, beacon, and air-to-ground ranging.

It was introduced on the Block 25 F-16C/F-16D in 1984, followed by the (V)4 version on Block 30s, and the (V)6 during the production run of the Block 40. Initial Block 50 and Block 52 deliveries, starting in 1991, used the APG-68(V5) with an advanced VHSIC (very high speed integrated circuit) programmable signal processor. International customers received the V(5), V(7) and V(8) versions.

The most advanced model of the APG-68 is the (V)9 which is installed on US Air Force and international Block 50 and Block 52 aircraft. The V(9) provides 30% greater detection range, search volume, tracking accuracy, reliability and resolution, improved supportability and enhanced growth potential. Its advanced processing techniques provide enhanced ECCM (electronic counter-countermeasures) capabilities and enable its synthetic aperture radar (SAR) mode to function correctly. The V(9) was upgraded after the Israeli Air Force reported problems with its performance.

The first production V(9) radars equipped the Hellenic Air Force Block 52+ aircraft delivered under the Peace Xenia IV programme. The (V)10, an improved version of the (V)9, offered a 33% increase in air-to-air detection range, improved reliability and an improved SAR mapping capability. Originally intended for 240 US Air Force Block 50, Block 52 and international aircraft, it has not entered production.

NORTHROP GRUMMAN APG-80

Introducing the agile beam technology for the AESA, the APG-80's development (which started as a 1,000-element AESA upgrade for the APG-68) was funded by the UAE to equip its Block 60 F-16E and F-16F Desert Falcon. The radars were delivered between 2003 and 2006. It requires more power than the APG-66 and APG-68 series and a water-cooled nose mounting. The APG-80 can simultaneously perform air-to-air search-and-track, air-to-ground targeting and aircraft terrain-following. It reportedly offers a search volume (140°), multi-tracking (20 tracks, six targets), detection range (50nm/95km against a one square metre (10.7ft^2) radar cross section target), high-resolution synthetic aperture radar imagery, and a two-fold increase in reliability compared to the APG-68.

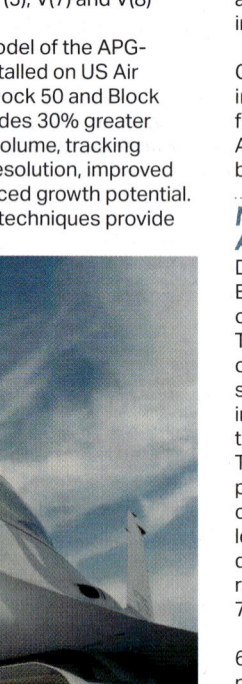
APG-80 Northrop Grumman

The APG-80 can cue the internal Northrop Grumman AAQ-32 FLIR (forward looking infrared) sensor which replaces the need for an externally-mounted pod such as the AAQ-28 Litening or the AAQ-33 Sniper used by other F-16s.

NORTHROP GRUMMAN APG-83 SABR

Despite cancellation of CAPES, the SABR Block 1.0 remained on schedule for delivery of the first of 150 radars and upgrade kits to Taiwan, starting in 2017. Lockheed Martin converted two prototypes at Fort Worth, a single-seat and a two-seat, which were flying in August 2014. Benefiting from the cachet that comes from its selection for the ongoing Taiwanese and cancelled CAPES upgrade programmes, Northrop Grumman said SABR offers up to five times better reliability than legacy radars, and leverages technology developed for their series-production AESA radars: the Lockheed Martin F-22's APG-77(V)1, APG-80, and the F-35's APG-81.

The SABR weighs less than the APG-68 MSA. Its single receiver-exciter and processor unit replaces two of the four LRUs (line replaceable units) in the APG-68 design. The SABR has a high level of commonality – Northrop Grumman says 95% – with the APG-81 software, which means future block upgrades developed for the F-35 can be incorporated. The SABR offers SAR capabilities with high resolution for areas of interest, and automatic target recognition and cueing. These include air-to-air detection

APG-68 Northrop Grumman

DB-110 Hellenic Air Force

mission, or as tasked in the air as the tactical scenario or mission changes.

A super wide field of view (SWFOV) low-altitude over-flight mid-wave infrared (MWIR) sensor was added.

Larry Maver, Business Development Director for the then UTC Aerospace Systems (now Collins Aerospace), outlined the key aspects of the third generation upgrade. "It's basically the same camera in terms of size, weight [and] power save the additional new features added which enhance capability," he said. "The most significant upgrade was to increase the image resolution by introducing new focal planes, the new third SWFOV which could be used below an altitude of 5,000ft [1,524m] and modernised avionics. Our objectives over time were for the camera to have selectable optical sub-systems which customers could use irrespective of whether they were flying at high altitudes [of] up to 50,000ft [15,240m], from long range [say 20 miles/32km] to look 70 miles [113km] away across a border, using the narrow field of view [NFOV] optics. A wide field of view [WFOV] optical system is used vertically or out to a distance of typically around 10 to 15 miles [16 to 24km]. The intention was to produce a pod that would fulfil all the different 'recce' mission types an air force would require with a single system."

Currently the Collins Aerospace third-generation system is the only one in the world providing users with a high-performance airborne reconnaissance capability comprising three fields-of-view within a single compact sensor. These are:
- *a 110in (2.8m) focal length VNIR NFOV channel and complementary 55in (1.4m) focal length mid-wave infrared NFOV channel;*
- *a 16in (410mm) focal length VNIR wide WFOV channel and complementary 14in (360mm) focal length MWIR WFOV channel and,*
- *a 2.5in (64mm) focal length MWIR Super Wide Field Of View (SWFOV) channel.*

In terms of sensor range and altitude, the NFOV, VNIR and MWIR sensors are typically used at altitudes between 20,000ft and 50,000ft (6,100m to 15,240m) for long-range stand-off missions where covert operations and aircrew and aircraft safety are the main priorities. As long as weather conditions are good, imaging quality capture by the NFOV is high anywhere between ten and 70 miles (16-113km approximately). For missions requiring image capture close to the aircraft's position, such as large area coverage or high altitude over-flight, the WFOV, VNIR and MWIR sensors will be used at altitudes between 5,000 and 20,000ft (1,524-6,140m) and for stand-off ranges between target over-flight and 30 miles (48km). The SWFOV capability comes into its own in low cloud overcast weather conditions or when the mission requires low-altitude imaging. This sensor has a 2.5in (64mm) MWIR which is optimised for operational heights below 5,000ft (1,524m).

The system's sensor and avionics suite is contained within the reconnaissance pod, which is designed to fit on the centreline of an F-16. The key features contained within the pod are:
- *Forward and aft data link antennae in the nose and tail sections;*
- *The DB-110 sensor/camera housed in the centre section of the pod behind the window shutter;*
- *Environmental Control System (ECS) and Temperature Control Unit (TCU) at both ends of the pod which cool, heat and protect the systems sensors and avionics during a mission, especially at altitudes around the maximum ceiling height;*
- *A single pneumatic window shutter assembly to protect the Oblique and Nadir windows. This window opens/closes automatically and manually as required during the mission;*

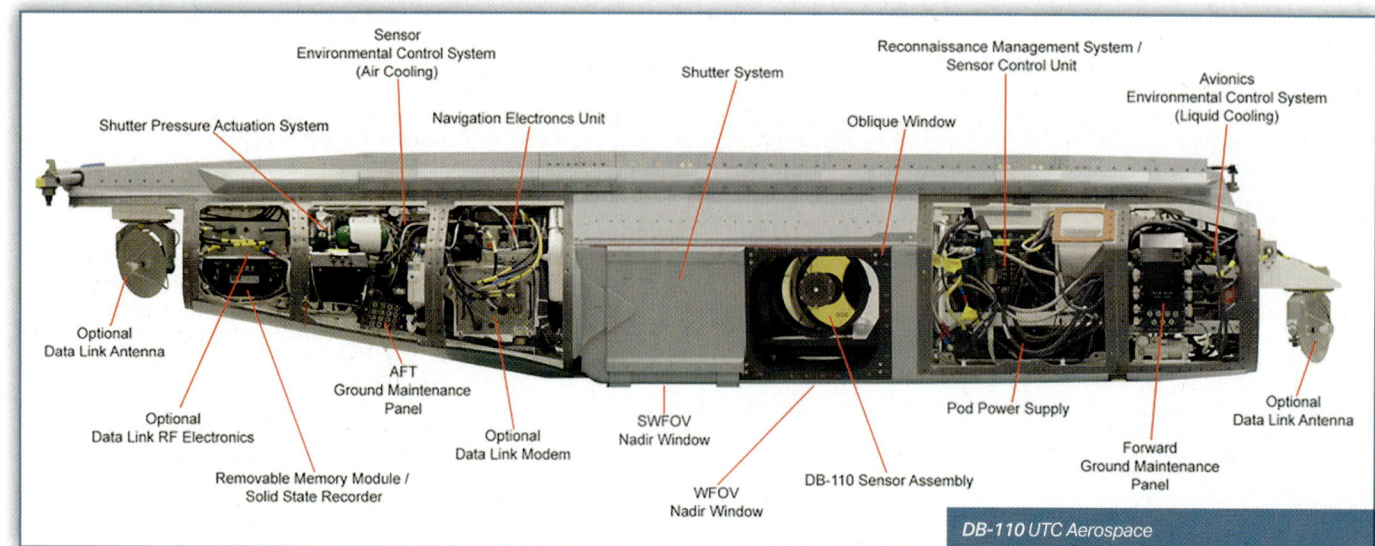
DB-110 UTC Aerospace

- Pod Power Supply (PPS) unit and Solid State Recorder (SSR) located in the forward and aft sections of the pod and the,
- Reconnaissance Management System (RMS) and Sensor Control Unit (SCU) located next to the PPS and,
- An Airborne Data Link Terminal (ADLT).

During data capture, the sensor uses visible and IR optics to limit image diffraction on the sensor's charged couple device and a two-axis image stabilisation process to compensate for the aircraft's motion and reduce image smear to sub-pixel level. The optical sensors certainly gather high-resolution, motion-free images of exceptional quality. This enables the system to operate up to a speed of Mach 1.6.

Autonomous operation of the pod's system is controlled by its reconnaissance management system (RMS) situated in the forward compartment between the camera and the forward ECS module. The RMS can manage both pre-planned and real-time collection tasks. Communication between the aircraft and the pod is achieved through the interface system contained within the aircraft's centreline. The system also uses the aircraft's MFD and the pilot's hands-on-throttle and stick (HOTAS) selections. The interface enables the pilot to view imagery of targets as required, image targets of opportunity that were not in the original plan and manage and monitor the system as a whole. Analysts located on the ground are provided with a status report for the mission, which enables them to monitor the aircraft's progress as it completes each imaging task. Aircrew can also interrogate

DB-110 Hellenic Air Force

the system during a mission using the SSR to retrieve imagery, assess it and if necessary, change the order in which subsequent tasks are completed.

AIM-9X SIDEWINDER

The AIM-9X Sidewinder, a supersonic air-to-air guided missile with full day/night capability, comprises six main components: missile body, a passive infrared (IR) target acquisition system, proportional navigational guidance, a closed-loop position fin actuator unit (FAU) and a target detector, warhead and rocket motor.

Propulsion is provided by a solid-propellant rocket motor which incorporates a manual safe-arm selector assembly. The missile is configured with an annular blast fragmentation warhead controlled by an electronic safe-arm device.

Aerodynamic lift and stability are provided by four forward-mounted fixed wings. Four fins, mounted in line with the fixed wings and activated by the FAU, manoeuvre the missile.

Manoeuvrability is enhanced by a jet vane control (JVC) that deflects the rocket motor thrust to aid turning, which is controlled by a tail actuation section.

A key benefit of the AIM-9X is its imaging focal plane array infrared sensor,

AIM-9X Raytheon

which has IR-counter countermeasures and has demonstrated very effective detection and tracking performance within visual and BVR engagement.

The AIM-9X incorporates new improvements integrated as part its spiral development. The Block II version includes an improved fuse and updated electronics – which enable lock-on after launch capability

AIM-9M MSgt Michael Ammons/US Air Force

14,590lb (64.9kN) and its maximum wet thrust with afterburner at 23,770lb (105.7kN).

The F100-220 also introduced another major upgrade, aimed at enhancing engine safety and reliability. Although the F100-200 retained the F100's traditional hydromechanical control system as a back-up, P&W gave the F100-220 a digital electronic engine control, along with an engine diagnostic unit to record in-flight engine performance data for maintenance and troubleshooting faults.

This "big step in innovation" allowed pilots of F100-powered aircraft to command unrestricted throttle movement and reduced their workload, according to Zotti.

When introducing the upgrades into new F100-220 engines, P&W also began producing -220E conversion kits by which any previously built F100-100 and F100-200 could be converted to F100-220 standard.

P&W's next step in developing the F100 was to introduce the F100-229 in 1989. This engine, which incorporated a new suite of durability advancements (among them new coatings for its HPT stages), offered a dry-thrust increase to 17,800lb (79kN) and maximum thrust with reheat of 29,160lb (129.7kN).

The F100-229, comparable in thrust to GE's F110-129 models, remains the standard F100 model offered for the F-16C, F-16D and F-15E Strike Eagle. However, in 2009 P&W began offering an F100-229 engine enhancement package (EEP), which parlayed technological advances developed for P&W's fifth-generation F119 and F135 fighter engines into a new suite of improvements for the F100.

THE F100-229EEP

These improvements, which included thermal barrier coatings and advanced materials in the F110-229EEP's combustor and HPT, were designed primarily to increase the engine's service interval between overhauls to 6,000 TACS. This increase of 40%, allowed each F100-229EP to remain on-wing for up to ten years between overhauls and offer 30% lower life-cycle costs. The F100 was the first fighter engine certified by the US Air Force for a 6,000-TAC interval.

The improvements also aimed to make "the components in the engine's compressor and turbine more supportable from a maintenance standpoint", according to Zotti. This enabled aircraft mechanics to replace "significantly more" compressor and turbine blades at operational bases, so fewer engines needed sending away for depot maintenance.

Zotti said the F100 continues to benefit from P&W's fifth-generation F119 and F135 sustainment and improvement programmes. "It's the only fourth-generation engine that can learn from two operational fifth-generation products," he said.

In addition to full-authority digital engine control, engine health monitoring and sensor technologies, and improved turbine coatings, the F100 programme also benefits from P&W's fifth-generation engine work on more damage-tolerant materials and advanced cooling schemes.

However, P&W's fifth-generation engines have also benefited from the F100 programme – and continue to do so. These benefits "are not necessarily from new technologies", said Zotti. Rather, "from early on, we learned what worked and what didn't work" in providing customer technical and logistical support, "and how to support a mixed-model family, in a variety of configurations, and a large customer base."

P&W's support for the F100 includes a continuous component improvement programme, which is funded by the engine family's many customers. On their behalf, "we look at reliability and maintainability drivers, and Pratt & Whitney looks at ways of improving the design," said Zotti.

SALES SUCCESS

Over time, P&W's improvements have made the F100 a major sales success. The company has now made more than 7,300 F100s, of which more than 3,800 remain in service. Zotti said P&W "supports the air forces of 23 countries" in operating F100 engines. Pratt & Whitney's F-16 latest customersare Romania, which purchased a batch of F-16s second-hand from Portugal, and Iraq which bought 36 Block 52 F-16IQs.

A PLACE IN HISTORY

According to the US Air Force Safety Statistics, the F100 is the safest US single-engine-fighter engine ever. It has also made history many times, even recently. On July 10, 2013 a non-afterburning F100-220U powered history's first arrested landing on an aircraft carrier by an unmanned aircraft, when a Northrop Grumman X-47B landed on the deck of the USS George H W Bush (CVN 77).

For this achievement Northrop Grumman, the US Navy, and the X-47B's development team won the National Aeronautic Association's 2013 Robert J Collier Trophy, US aviation's most prestigious award. In April, the same aircraft-engine combination successfully conducted the world's first fully autonomous aerial refuelling, off the coast of Maryland.

On July 27, 2022, Pratt & Whitney commemorated 50 years of service for the F100 engine, which had accumulated more than 30 million engine flight hours.

In late December 2022, the Hermeus Corporation, an American startup company based in Atlanta, Georgia focused on the development of commercial hypersonic aircraft, selected the Pratt & Whitney F100 turbofan to act as the turbine portion of its turbine-based combined cycle (TBCC) engine. Named Chimera II, the TBCC engine is a hybrid between a turbine engine and a ramjet that enables both low-speed and high-speed operation.

Chimera II is the powerplant for the Hermeus Darkhorse hypersonic uncrewed aerial system with multi-mission flexibility and is fully reusable.
Chris Kjelgaard

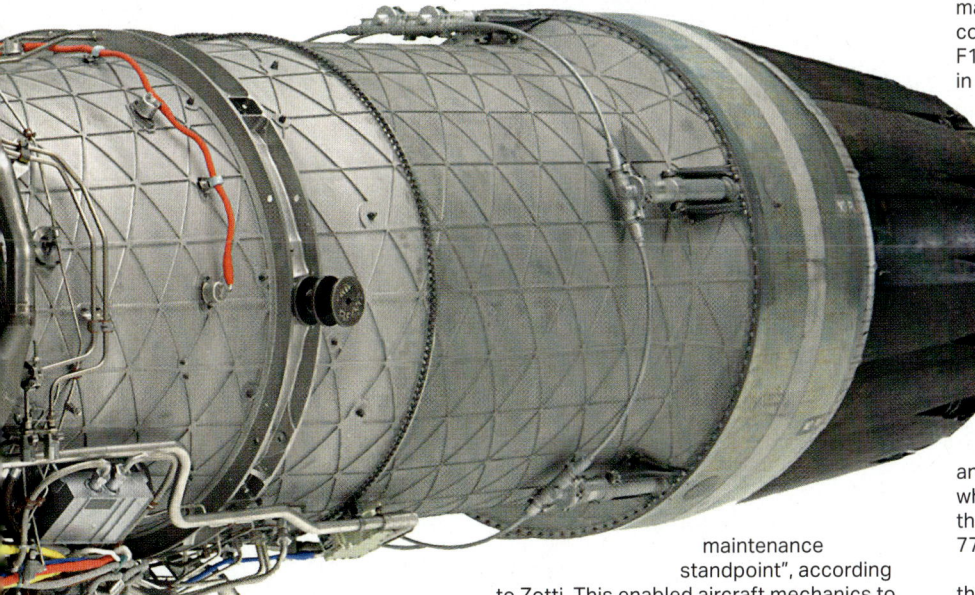

F-16 Falcon Still in the Fight

Proud Heritage,

The GE Aviation F110-GE-132 turbofan engine rated at 32,500lb of thrust is used by the UAEAF Block 60 F-16E and F-16F fleet. All images GE Aviation

Originally developed in the early 1980s for the US Navy to offer a much higher-thrust alternative for the insufficiently powerful Pratt & Whitney TF30-P-414As powering the navy's F-14A Tomcats, GE Aviation's F110 engine began life as the F101X, a derivative of the F101-102 turbofan the company developed for the Rockwell B-1B bomber.

Renamed the F110, the derivative turbofan – whose core is virtually identical to those of the B-1B's F101-102, the KC-135's CFM56-2 and the B-2A's F118-101 engines – was suitable in terms of developmental maturity and thrust capability to break the monopoly position on US fighter aircraft that Pratt & Whitney had secured in the 1970s.

The F110 did so when the US Air Force launched its Alternative Fighter Engine programme (commonly known in US military circles as the 'Great Engine War') in 1984. The aim of the programme was to find an engine that not only could reduce maintenance costs compared with the P&W-manufactured F100-100 and F100-200 engines powering the air force's F-15s and F-16s, but also provide more thrust.

P&W's early F100-100 engines offered only 900 total accumulated cycles (TACs) between overhauls and the US Air Force also regarded the F100-200 as being insufficiently reliable.

While P&W later fixed these problems with the F100-220, it did so in the knowledge that the GE F110 was by then winning volume orders on the F-16 and F-15E Strike Eagle and offered 3,000 TACs on-wing before overhaul.

GE made the F110 available initially for the US Air Force as the F110-100, which provided 28,000lb (125kN) of thrust with reheat for Block 30 and Block 40 F-16s and as the F110-400 for the US Navy, which offered a similar thrust level for the F-14B and F-14D.

The F110 had three fan stages, nine high-pressure compressor stages, an annular combustor, a single high-pressure turbine stage and two low-pressure turbine stages.

Subsequently GE Aviation developed the F110 design to offer a more powerful version, the F110-129. This engine, which produces 29,400lb (131kN) of thrust, won business on the F-15E Strike Eagle and also on Block 50 F-16Cs and F-16Ds and remains widely in service today, as does the F110-100.

The next – and still latest – part of the F110 thrust-growth effort was GE's development of the F110-132, a new F110 version powering the 80 Block 60 F-16s ordered by the United Arab Emirates Air Force.

Employing a radial rather than a spray-bar augmentor and incorporating durability improvements (including three one-piece 'blisks' to provide all three rotor stages in its fan module), the F110-132 produces 32,500lb (144.6kN) of thrust and offers a service life of 4,300 TACs, even in the harsh desert environment of the UAE.

IMPROVING F110 RELIABILITY

Joe Guenther, general manager of GE Aviation's F101, F110 and F118 family of engines, who also has customer-service responsibility for all military-operated versions of GE's commercial engines, said GE's next major development effort for the F110 programme was to improve its on-wing reliability further.

After initially increasing F110-100 and F110-129 on-wing reliability to 4,000 TACs and 4,300 TACS respectively, GE began developing a Service Life Extension Program (SLEP) for the F110-129. This increased this engine's on-wing reliability to 6,000 TACs – effectively extending its time-on-wing between major overhauls from seven to ten years.

How GE did so is interesting. Guenther said that, using "appropriate rights" it owned as an equal partner with Snecma in the CFM International joint venture, GE "leveraged technology from the CFM56-7" – the world's most-common commercial turbofan engine – to provide a series of durability and reliability-related upgrades for the F110-129 core.

These included improvements in the 3-D aerodynamics of the F110-129's compressor airflow (to increase efficiency as well as rotor and structure life); adding cooling channels in the combustor, doubling its service life; aerodynamic, materials and cooling changes in its turbine blades and stages, increasing durability; and modifying the augmentor design, to increase durability, reduce maintenance and improve maintainability. The US Government paid for qualification of the modification of the original F110-129 design into the new F110-129 SLEP configuration.

According to Guenther, development of the SLEP core for the F110-129 turned "a somewhat unique [F110] core" into "an identical bill of materials" for any engine in the F101, F110-129 and F118 family.

This commonality potentially allows the US Air Force to buy a SLEP upgrade kit and "put it into any engine they need it for", among the three engine models. GE is now producing SLEP kits for the F101 and expects to deliver the first one in late 2015, for installation in an operational F101-102 engine in early 2016.

GE then fed the SLEP advances it developed for the F110-129 back into improving the CFM56-2 engines powering almost all US Air Force C-135-family aircraft,

F-16 Falcon Still in the Fight

Proud Future

as well as the US Navy's E-6B Mercury airborne command-post jets.

It did so in a CFM Propulsion Upgrade Program – called C-PUP by the US Air Force – involving CFM International and the US Air Force.

Subsequently, GE self-funded development of a SLEP upgrade for the F110-100 to provide a 6,000-TAC interval between overhauls and is awaiting qualification for this modification by the US Air Force.

Guenther said "some international customers have expressed interest" in the increased-life F110-100 SLEP modification for retrofit in their existing F-16s. They include Greece, Israel and Turkey – "and if the US Air Force wanted, it could have it too."

He said GE's SLEP development effort for the F110-100 identified areas in the engine that couldn't be modified easily – mainly its low-pressure turbine module – and "basically newly designed" them, creating an engine which "is very like the F110-129".

THE F110 COMPONENT IMPROVEMENT PROGRAMME

Separate from GE's SLEP development efforts is a continuing F110 Component Improvement Program (CIP), in which the US Air Force is providing $30-35 million to keep improving the engine's durability and reduce its maintenance and management workload.

Although the F110 already demonstrates "world-class reliability", according to Guenther – who said some examples have already exceeded the engine's design life in service – the CIP effort will keep US Air Force F110s in service for many years to come.

GE is drawing upon its commercial-engine development work for F110 CIP inspiration, including work on new turbine and combustor designs to improve durability and reliability for operations in hot and harsh environments. From work on the GE90 and other large commercial engines, "we're learning that certain [blade] geometries and cooling schemes work better than others," said

The GE Aviation F110-GE-129 turbofan engine rated at 29,000lb of thrust is subject to a Component Improvement Programme.

Guenther.

One result is that the latest F110 turbine blades have "very similar features to the latest GE90 turbine blades", even though they are much smaller. According to Guenther, GE is also feeding design-improvement experience from its commercial and F110 programmes back into CIPs for other engines, such as the T700, F404 and F414.

Two other F110 CIP improvements are worth noting. One has changed the design of the F110-129 fuel nozzle, which incorporated safety wire meant to lock it into position to make the design safer but later proved to require more maintenance than the nozzle in the F110-100.

The change has introduced a "molar fitting", which allows locking of the F110-129 fuel nozzle into position but doesn't require any safety wire, reducing the maintenance requirement.

Also, GE's continuing engineering efforts to address operating capabilities in hot and harsh environments include modernising the F110-132's control system to provide full-authority digital engine control, which the F110-129 already has. This will address any potential F110-132 obsolescence issues.

SALES TO DATE

In September 2019, GE Aerospace's F110 family of engines surpassed 10 million flight hours. The F110 powers almost 70% of the most advanced US Air Force F-16 aircraft, and F-16 fleets in Bahrain, Chile, Egypt, Greece, Israel, Oman, Turkey, and United Arab Emirates. In recent years, Lockheed Martin has received orders for new Advanced F-16s from Bahrain, Bulgaria, Jordan, Morocco, the Phillippines, Slovakia, and Taiwan. Over 100 aircraft will be Block 70 models powered by GE Aerospace F110 engines including those for Bahrain, Bulgaria, Slovakia and Taiwan.

The F110 also powers Japan's F-2 indigenous fighter and many of the Advanced Boeing F-15 Eagles delivered in the past 19 years. Newest F110 variants have gone through GE Aerospace's Service Life Extension Program (SLEP). SLEP hardware upgrades include three-dimensional aerodynamic technology plus upgrades to the combustor and high-pressure turbine.

In addition, GE provides engine overhaul support to the US Air Force through a programme called Pacer Phantom. To date, 3,400 F110 engines have been ordered worldwide of which 1,676 power F-16 fighters. ***Chris Kjelgaard***

The Viper

Mark Ayton spoke with Lockheed Martin's F-16 chief engineer, Mike McSpadden, about the Viper upgrade.

Starting this explanatory feature about the Viper upgrade it's appropriate to start with a few facts, which may surprise you. You can find the F-16V term used in countless features posted on websites all over the internet in reference to advanced variants of the F-16. However, the term F-16V does not denote a variant of the jet but an avionics upgrade configuration. The term is used by Lockheed Martin as a marketing indicator just like fifth generation, another slogan so effectively used to refer to its F-22 and F-35 fighter aircraft.

Any F-16A, F-16B, F-16C or F-16D fitted with the Viper upgrade retains its original production designation, so a Block 20 F-16A or F-16B with the Viper upgrade remains a Block 20 F-16A or F-16B.

Lockheed Martin's marketeers opted to name the avionics upgrade Viper because the name has been used by F-16 pilots to refer to the aircraft for decades, even though its official name is the Fighting Falcon.

ORIGIN
The Viper upgrade started with a retrofit programme for the Republic of China Air Force comprising a package of systems centred around a new avionics suite, an AESA radar, and Operational Flight Program (OFP) software V1. Additional requirements from other customers led to follow-on configurations with V2 and V3 OFP software.

Lockheed Martin made further improvements which were introduced on new build aircraft and are now offered in retrofit. Mike McSpadden, Lockheed Martin's F-16 chief engineer described the procedure as "a continual improvement process that builds on itself."

Explaining the process, McSpadden said: "Every time we gain a new F-16 customer, we add capabilities to the aircraft, and in most cases those capabilities are retrofittable to older aircraft. We normally call the retrofit configuration the F-16 Viper upgrade, which is a package that includes an AESA radar, but there are other upgrades for the F-16 that don't include an AESA radar. But the F-16 Viper upgrade is different to a new-build Block 70 which has similar avionics but an airframe with a 12,000-hour service life, and improvements to the airframe and some mechanical systems."

F-16 VIPER UPGRADE
The heart and soul of the Viper upgrade is a new state of the art AESA radar. More specifically the Northrop Grumman APG-83, a radar system that can conduct near simultaneous air-to-air and air-to-ground modes, which generates a lot of information for the pilot.

Discussing the upgrade, McSpadden said: "We had to upgrade the core computers to process the information. So, we upgraded the mission computer, the display generator and the up-front control computer which provides upfront control for the pilot. Given the amount of information generated by the AESA radar and the sensors, we also incorporated a 6 x 8in high-definition centre pedestal display. To handle the amount of information and distribute it between new mission computers, sensors and displays we installed a Gigabit Ethernet to supplement the legacy 1553 data bus. Ethernet is like a communication superhighway.

"We undertook a lot of work to ensure the RF interface between the AESA radar and the electronic warfare systems are compatible. This was accomplished by integrating the new Viper Shield electronic warfare system. We also integrated an improved datalink and a new helmet mounted display."

These systems are part of the initial new build Block 70 aircraft configuration, but further system improvements were introduced as Lockheed Martin gained more Block 70 customers. The company has already improved the Block 70 baseline OFP software which is offered in the Viper upgrade configuration. According to McSpadden, "it's like the second generation of the Viper upgrade."

He gave an example: "In production, we are in the process of implementing the new Common Digital Flight Control Computer 2 which has an advanced flight management system featuring an enhanced autopilot, auto throttle, and deep stall recovery. These improvements were possible thanks to the greater memory and throughput to the flight control computer. Now we can offer that same upgrade in retrofit."

Republic of China Air Force Block 20 F-16A 6601 (c/n TA-1) wearing its US Air Force serial number 93-0702/ED (allocated as part of the foreign military sale process) was the first single-seat aircraft to be upgraded with the Viper upgrade. Post upgrade, the aircraft remains a Block 20 F-16A. Lockheed Martin

Upgrade

KEEPING APACE WITH THE USAF

Discussing the different phases of the Viper upgrade, McSpadden explained that each customer has a unique set of requirements. "A retrofit usually starts with a baseline configuration, so the kit we supply is tailored to the customer's baseline. For example, one customer wanted a new helmet mounted display, which was subsequently integrated for a follow-on customer together with a new data link. Configuration characteristics unique to each customer, though the respective aircraft will look about the same."

As the largest operator of the F-16, how the US Air Force configures its aircraft tends to lead the configuration choices of FMS customers.

For example, the F-16 Viper upgrade bought by numerous FMS customers has numerous similarities to the US Air Force F-16 upgrade. In fact, Lockheed Martin makes FMS F-16 configurations as common to the US Air Force F-16 configuration as possible, including those modified with the Viper upgrade.

The Defense Security Cooperation Agency states that major FMS programmes nurture long-term relationships with the US military, including access to joint training and doctrine and increased opportunities for interoperability with US forces.

US Air Force F-16s are being modified under a programme led by a team named the Post Block Integration Team. The team is part of the Air Force Life Cycle Management Center's Fighters and Advanced Aircraft Directorate.

The US Air Force programme involves 608 Block 40 and Block 50 F-16 aircraft. Each one will undergo up to 22 modifications designed to improve lethality and ensure effectiveness for meeting current and future threats. Modifications include the APG-83 AESA radar, an upgraded mission computer to almost the same configuration used for the Viper upgrade, Link-16 datalink, cockpit modernisation, a high-speed data bus, a new electronic warfare system, a new centre pedestal display, a programmable data generator, and communication system upgrades. Installation of some modifications have already started and will continue over several years.

A structural upgrade programme called SLEP (service life extension programme) provides each US Air Force Block 40 and Block 50 F-16 aircraft with a 13,000-hour service life.

McSpadden noted that the US Air Force upgrade programmes are designed to keep its F-16s flying until the 2045-2048 which also serves as a confidence builder for FMS partners.

RETROFITS

To date, all Viper upgrade retrofits have been completed in the recipient customer nation using a kit shipped by Lockheed Martin. A kit comprises several packages which are delivered to the recipient nation's depot. Components in each package are installed on the aircraft in accordance with the work instruction card. Tools supplied with the kit are used to ensure components and parts are installed in the right location. Lockheed Martin also provides technical assistance.

Detailing the process, McSpadden said: "Some nations opt to undertake upgrades indigenously to their air force, with the kits installed at its depot, Alternately, the air force can choose to nominate a company to undertake the work. Sometimes Lockheed Martin contracts with either the air force or the company. Other times, the recipient nation's Ministry of Defence contracts with the company, which then installs the kits. In almost every instance, Lockheed Martin provides some kind of technical support to help overcome any issues with the installation.

"We normally undertake what we call a kit proof for the first two aircraft, usually an F-16A and an F-16B or an F-16C and an F-16D. We also have a lot of people onsite to support the first kit installations. We also conduct a lot of training, so the air force or industry technicians understand how to read the plans, the work instruction cards, where the parts go, and how to use the tools. The technicians learn lessons and then start upgrading a second and third aircraft, performing more of the hands-on work themselves."

Four countries are currently flying aircraft with the Viper upgrade installed and each of those four nations continue to install F-16 Viper upgrade kits to their remaining aircraft.

F-16 Falcon Still in the Fight

An artist's rendering used for promotion of the F-16 Viper upgrade. Lockheed Martin

VIPER UPGRADE TEST PROGRAMME

Lockheed Martin designs an upgrade kit to meet the customer's requirements which goes through a series of different system engineering design reviews. Handling-quality simulator testing of the avionics package is conducted at Lockheed Martin's Fort Worth facility.

Lockheed Martin modifies a flight test aircraft using either a production engineering specification or a flight test engineering specification and loads the appropriate OFP software.

Once functional check flights are completed by Lockheed Martin test pilots, the aircraft is/are flown to Edwards Air Force Base, California for assignment to the 416th Flight Test Squadron. A component of the 412th Test Wing, the 416th is the Air Force Test Center's developmental test squadron for fighters.

The 416th tests all F-16s, US Air Force, FMS, new-build or upgraded for suitability of flying, maintenance, and engineering. A test team assigned to the 416th creates the run cards which list the specifics of how a system will be assessed. During flight test missions, instrumentation installed on the aircraft collects data which is analysed by both Lockheed Martin and the US Air Force.

The F-16 Viper upgrade flight test programme has remained active since the first two Republic of China Air Force (Taiwanese) aircraft arrived at Edwards in October 2015. The programme has tested jets from all FMS F-16 Viper upgrade customers.

Taiwan was the first F-16 Viper upgrade customer. The Republic of China Air Force is already operating the Viper upgrade configuration and continues to modify its remaining aircraft. In addition, Lockheed Martin is completing further work on a couple of Taiwanese aircraft which are currently being prepared for a flight test programme of new capabilities.

The Hellenic Air Force Viper upgrade programme involved the modification of one aircraft at Fort Worth followed by flight testing by the 416th Flight Test Squadron at Edwards.

VIPER BASIC, VIPER PLUS

The first iteration of the Viper upgrade was called Viper basic. This standard was followed by Viper plus which features the advanced cockpit, the standby flight instrument, changes to the centre pedestal display, electronic gauges, the new common digital flight control computer with autopilot and auto-throttle, a new helmet-mounted display, and changes to some of the core computers. A Viper plus cockpit looks like the latest version of the Block 70.

Since the first Block 1 F-16s entered service with the US Air Force in 1978, those jets and each subsequent Block has operated with an M-series OFP software. M denotes mission computer. When Lockheed Martin introduced its Viper upgrade the baseline OFP was M6, the so-called launch standard for the Viper upgrade. The company changed is OFP designation nomenclature to the V-series. V1 and V2 were developed for retrofit programmes, as was V3 which recently went into production on the first Block 70 aircraft. Some aircraft retrofitted with V3 are in service. V4 is a production configuration still in development and will also be offered as a Viper upgrade.

In general, a new customer receives the latest OFP when they order a Viper upgrade except for V4 which is currently in development. V4 runs the Common Digital Flight Control Computer 2, the advanced cockpit, and provisions for a baseline IRST capability. The Common Digital Flight Control Computer 2 is in development for the new-build Block 70. Similarly, the existing baseline IRST capability is being modified for the new-build Block 70, and Viper Shield will eventually be retrofitted on the first Block 70 aircraft built.

According to McSpadden, Lockheed Martin has future capabilities in work continuing its evolution in both retrofit and new production, more than 46 years since the first F-16 rolled out of the Fort Worth plant.

Republic of Korea Air Force Block 52 F-16D 92-4046 (c/n KD-18) in US Air Force markings over the precision impact range area at Edwards Air Force Base, California. The aircraft was assigned to the Edwards-based 416th Flight Test Squadron in support of the Republic of Korea's F-16 Viper upgrade programme. US Air Force/Ethan Wagner

F-16 Falcon Still in the Fight

A promotional photo issued by Lockheed Martin showing a theoretical weapon load-out on an F-16 with the Viper upgrade. The aircraft is shown with triple ejector racks on stations 3 and 7 and hextuple ejector racks on stations 4 and 6. Lockheed Martin

F-16 Falcon Still in the Fight

Royal Bahrain Air Force Block 70 F-16D 1611 over Edwards Air Force Base, California, on its delivery flight from Donaldson Center Airport, Greenville, South Carolina on March 28, 2023. US Air Force/412th Test Wing

Block 70

Mark Ayton spoke with Lockheed Martin's F-16 chief engineer, Mike McSpadden, about the latest Block 70 version.

ALQ-254 VIPER SHIELD ELECTRONIC WARFARE SYSTEM

The Block 70 F-16 is equipped with a new electronic warfare system called Viper Shield built by L3 Harris.

Viper Shield provides a virtual electronic shield around the aircraft which is designed to protect the aircraft in complex battlespaces with improved probability of intercept against agile threats. The sensors that feed the system are embedded at locations around the fuselage to enable 360° spherical coverage.

Use of an all-digital architecture enables a smaller form factor, reduced weight and allows for future upgrades.

Similarly, use of software-defined components enables a digital radar warning receiver (DRWR) and digital countermeasure capabilities in a fully integrated, internally mounted system, and a digital radio frequency memory (DRFM)-based jamming system helps to protect the aircraft from advanced threats. The DRWR is integrated with the system's jammers.

Viper Shield is designed to operate with the Northrop Grumman APG-83 AESA radar for RF compatibility, provides the pilot with a level of situational awareness greater than earlier Block F-16 aircraft, operates in active and passive mode, and has a dedicated multifunction display.

The system comprises fewer critical components than previous generation electronic warfare systems which results in a smaller form factor, reduced weight, and a higher mean time between failure and lower lifecycle costs. Modular design allows maintainers to swap line replaceable units (LRUs) in the field.

L3 Harris is developing Viper Shield in partnership with the US Air Force and Lockheed Martin. *L3 Harris*

Notable in this promotional photo of a Block 70 F-16D is the Legion-ES Infrared Search and Track sensor, a new capability for the F-16 aircraft. *Lockheed Martin*

McSpadden said the increased service life is based on test results, "the US Air Force took a very low-hour Block 50 F-16 out of service which was used by Lockheed Martin for durability testing. The aircraft was placed in a full-scale durability test fixture and tested for over 27,000 equivalent flight hours. We could have a certified service life based on half of that figure, so for the Block 70 we could have gone to 13,000 hours but opted for 12,000 as the certified service life for the Block 70."

According to a US Air Force press release issue on November 3, 2015: "The Block 50 F-16C was tested to 27,713 equivalent flight hours (EFH) during 32 rounds of comprehensive stress tests at Lockheed Martin's Full Scale Durability Test facility in Fort Worth. The airframe was then subjected to several maximum-load conditions to demonstrate that the airframe still had sufficient strength to operate within its full operational flight envelope."

The aircraft then entered the teardown inspection and fractography phase of the test programme. Test data, collected over nearly two years, was used to identify an extended, definitive flight hour limit for the F-16 Fighting Falcon and demonstrate the safety and durability of the aircraft well beyond its original design service life.

The durability test results were used to help design and verify Service Life Extension Program (SLEP) structural modifications for post-Block 40 F-16s and to support F-16 service life certification to at least 12,000 EFH. The SLEP is designed to extend the service life of Block 40/42 and Block 50/52 aircraft.

Explaining, McSpadden said: "In the durability testing, we found 26 areas that needed improvement to get the 12,000 hours in addition to modifications completed by the US Air Force under its F-16 structural life extension programme. For the Block 70, instead of adding a stiffener or a doubler, or a structural component to deal with those areas, we built them into the bulkhead. For example, the aircraft needed a thicker web machined into the bulkhead. All 26 areas requiring modification were incorporated in the production."

Improving the structure of the aircraft is one engineering aspect, but what about the use of composite materials on the new F-16? Mike McSpadden confirmed that Lockheed Martin is working with the US Air Force on the development of a new composite horizontal stabiliser which weighs 60lb less than the original components, "that's of benefit given the growth in weight of the improved engines."

F-16 Falcon Still in the Fight

Moving to Greenville

F-16 Falcon Still in the Fight

F-16D EB-1 moves from hangar 16 to the paint booth. Lockheed Martin

Just imagine winning an order requiring the production of 16 wooden kitchen tables and being asked to move your existing production facility to a location 1,000 miles away before production work can start. Challenging in some ways, but not the most complicated move to undertake. Now imagine winning an order requiring the production of the same number of F-16 fighter aircraft under the same arrangement. That's a challenge.

After more than 47 years of F-16 production at Air Force Plant 4 at Fort Worth, Texas, in 2017 Lockheed Martin decided to do just that. At the time, the company was expecting F-16 production to come to an end and was planning for F-35 production to ramp-up. The Fort Worth facility needed additional floor space for F-35 production.

Caleb Hendrick, director of F-16 production operations described the transition as a move that considered the F-16 as much as the F-35. "We had 16 F-16s to build. Fort Worth was quickly running out of space. Lockheed Martin evaluated potential sites, but ultimately Greenville was selected. It was considered a sustainment site and a low-cost centre from where Lockheed Martin could build the most affordable F-16. In short, F-16 production [16 Block 70 F-16s for Bahrain] at Greenville,

F-16D EB-1 in the paint booth. Lockheed Martin

An F-16 wing built by Israel Aerospace Industries being unboxed for F-16D EB-1. Lockheed Martin

Mark Ayton spoke with Lockheed Martin representatives about setting-up an F-16 production line at its Greenville, South Carolina facility.

Lockheed Martin production mechanics work on a centre fuselage section. Lockheed Martin

A Lockheed Martin production mechanic work on the forward fuselage section of Slovakian F-16C EA-1. Lockheed Martin

ramp-up F-35 production at Fort Worth and ride the F-16 programme into its sunset."

The announcement to move F-16 production to Greenville and use the available space to set up a production line was made in February 2017. The final F-16 built at the Fort Worth facility (Iraqi Air Force Block 52 F-16C serial number 1636 c/n RA-28), rolled off the production line in September 2017. It departed Naval Air Station Joint Reserve Base, Fort Worth on November 14, 2017.

As aircraft RA-28 moved through final assembly at Fort Worth, the process of dismantling the production line started. Over 4,000 project-related items and tools had to be crated up with an inventory and shipped to the existing facilities at Greenville. Shipping took 195 semi-tractor trailers.

INCREASE IN DEMAND
Demand for the F-16 increased after the decision to move to Greenville had been made. Explaining, Jeff Vernon, the company's build team senior manager said: "With the increase in production demand, Lockheed Martin ran models to determine the capacity of the Greenville plant with the space available. The modelling showed we could run the Greenville plant at the same pace as Fort Worth through the sunset years, with a monthly production rate of four aircraft."

Caleb Hendrick cited timing as the key factor in setting up the Greenville plant and maximising its capacity: "Fort Worth had plenty of capacity to run flow and had the space to optimise tools and people around the aeroplane from a manufacturing standpoint. Greenville's two hangars and facilities are not equivalent to the Fort Worth facility."

The decision was a cognisant point, with a finite production run and the uncertainties of achieving that in a sub-optimised space. Financially, the decision made sense for Bahrain and Lockheed Martin for closing out the programme at that time.

Hendrick continued: "Post decision and the move to Greenville, we realised there was a big demand for the Block 70 F-16 beyond the Bahraini contract. But could we meet demand with our production capacity at Greenville? With the number of aircraft we have to build at this point of the programme, it wouldn't be affordable to build a new facility. Therefore, the decision was made to optimise the space in hangar 16, maximise its capacity to four aircraft per month, and leverage co-production partners to produce major components to help augment space challenges and meet demand. This strategy also builds robustness within the production system versus relying solely on one manufacturing source from start to finish.

"We're working to get to four a month. When we delivered the first Block 70 aircraft to Bahrain, counting the forward and centre fuselages, and mated aeroplanes, we had 37 assemblies in work and 25 aircraft at different stages of assembly. We build the forward and centre fuselage sections from scratch at Greenville, and we mate the aft fuselage which comes from Hellenic Aerospace Industries in Greece."

HAND-BUILT AND TOOL-CONTROLLED
The F-16 remains a hand-built, tool-controlled aircraft. The Greenville facility is using the frames and tooling from the Fort Worth facility

Lockheed Martin production mechanics work on a centre fuselage section of Slovakian F-16C EA-1. Lockheed Martin

F-16 Falcon Still in the Fight

An early shot of the Greenville F-16 production line. Lockheed Martin

Lockheed Martin production mechanics walk with F-16D EB-1 under tow from the assembly line. Lockheed Martin

which are set out slightly differently to adhere to space constraints. Aircraft assembly at Greenville follows a rate station build process versus an end-to-end manufacturing line similar to Fort Worth. Each forward and centre fuselage section stays in its build area until it's 100% complete, then it's moved to be mated.

Explaining, Caleb Hendrick said: "We had to compress it a little bit, so the flow is not as optimal as you would have in a large factory, but the tools and the way we build the aircraft remain the same. We're adding in automation. For example, at the end of this year, we're adding an auto drill for the centre fuselage, it's going to drill several thousand holes that are currently hand drilled, as they were in Fort Worth. There are also several technological insertion projects being considered to improve the span of the production process."

IMPACTS ON PRODUCTION

The Greenville facility suffered supply chain delays primarily with major sub-assemblies lasting several months which occurred as Lockheed Martin was setting up its production line during the height of the COVID-19 pandemic.

According to Caleb Hendrick: "The programme established a schedule of record to reduce impacts associated with the pandemic. We loaded the first fuselage section on November 11, 2019, and drilled the first holes thereafter. A few months after, the COVID pandemic hit which affected the manufacturing and assembly process, but not as significantly as might be expected," he said.

Jeff Vernon said the facility followed the CDC recommendations and protocols of spacing, safe distances and those for people who came down with symptoms who went into quarantine. "We had sanitation

Production mechanics lower the cockpit section of F-16D EB-1 into position. Lockheed Martin

F-16D EB-1 inside the final assembly building. Lockheed Martin

stations in place, clean areas, shields, anything to minimise the impact on our workforce."

Hendrick described the timing of the production line set-up as somewhat fortuitous: "We were at low-rate production involving just a few assemblies in work and a small workforce, so when COVID broke out its impact was not as complicated as other Lockheed Martin facilities. The bulk of workforce growth took place after the height of COVID. To give you a sense of growth in our workforce, in January 2022 we had about 100 people on the assembly line, today we have over 450. At the time we had a handful of assemblies in work. Today, we have numerous aircraft in final assembly with some getting powered up, so the building has filled-up and the pace of work is frenetic. We anticipate the scope of assembly activity to increase a little bit more, and we're fast approaching all stations being filled-up.

"In terms of touch labour, we started in Greenville with a new workforce, very few

Lockheed Martin production mechanics stand ready to help with the mating process of the left wing to EB-1. Lockheed Martin

Lockheed Martin production mechanics carefully position the left-wing in place for mating to F-16D EB-1. Lockheed Martin

The left wing being lifted into position for mating to F-16D EB-1. Lockheed Martin

people came from Fort Worth, though in the past year we've relied heavily on expertise from our quality engineering community and a lot of the manufacturing experts based at Fort Worth. Subject matter experts who oversaw the production of thousands of F-16s are working as consultants in parts of the build process: structure and wiring are two examples. Most of the mechanics, technicians and electricians are new and not all of them have F-16 experience. Many of them are former crew chiefs and maintainers that worked on the F-16, so they know the platform, but they knew little about the actual production of the aircraft."

PRODUCTION FLOW

The aircraft's assembly to the point when the wheels and the vertical tail are fitted and all the systems are installed is completed in hangar 16, the major assembly hangar. The aircraft is then towed to a different building about a quarter of a mile away. This second building is used for final assembly which includes fitting the wings and numerous minor assemblies. The aircraft is switched on for the first time in the final assembly building and its systems are checked for full functionality. Before painting, the aircraft is checked for leaks and all the systems are run for the first time. This includes the pumps, the filtration systems to make sure there's nothing

F-16 Falcon Still in the Fight

Lockheed Martin production mechanics edge the left-wing into position for mating to F-16D EB-1. Lockheed Martin

contained in the fuel system or the tanks, and the aerial refuelling system and pumps.

Next stop is final painting, after which the aircraft is towed to flight operations for checking of the emergency power systems. Finally, the engine is started and run for the first time. This is the aircraft's final stop before its first and subsequent acceptance check flights.

Lockheed Martin test pilots based at Fort Worth travel to Greenville to conduct the acceptance check flights. According to Caleb Hendrick two Lockheed Martin test pilots travelled to Greenville to complete four acceptance check flights of the first jet, EB-1. One US Air Force pilot assigned to the Defense Contract Management Agency also took part, flying two further flights. Commenting,

Just inches to go before the left wing is attached to the fuselage of F-16D EB-1. Lockheed Martin

Hendrick said: "The data set from the flights showed that the new Block 70 configuration performed exceptionally well. Each of the Block 70 components, software, wiring, systems, and sub-systems performed as expected."

When the team checked over aircraft EB-1 after final assembly was complete, they encountered the kinds of teething issues expected with a first aircraft tool-controlled and built by hand. The lessons learned from EB-1 will improve the manufacturing process.

Hendrick said he is already seeing the production teams follow a comparable learning curve on each of the other aircraft currently in work, to EB-1. Concluding, he said: "What stood out as unique in terms of quality was the jet's performance. We completed some minor test operation adjustments which are standard for a first flight, but the aircraft landed in exceptional condition after each functional check flight which was backed-up by the data set. We didn't have to fly any extra flights, which was encouraging."

Support stands in place; Lockheed Martin production mechanics complete the left-wing mate to F-16D EB-1. Lockheed Martin

F-16 Falcon Still in the Fight

X-62A VISTA

Mark Ayton and Scott Dworkin provide an overview of the NF-16D VISTA, now designated the X-62A.

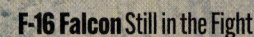

The United States Air Force Test Pilot School's Variable Stability In-flight Simulator Test Aircraft (VISTA) is a one-of-a-kind research and training vehicle developed jointly by the USAF Research Laboratory and Calspan Corporations Aerospace Group.

The VISTA provides developmental research, risk reduction testing and in-flight simulation capabilities for flight control system and cockpit display research and development. Because it can be configured to fly and behave like virtually any aircraft, from an unmanned aircraft to a C-17, it can be used to demonstrate advanced flight control system concepts to test pilots, RPA test pilots, combat systems operators and flight test engineers.

The aircraft is maintained and operated by Calspan personnel for the US Air Force Test Pilot School (TPS) at Edwards Air Force Base, California. The aircraft provides training for students in a wide range of handling and flying qualities and flight test techniques. VISTA also continues to provide developmental research, risk reduction and in-flight simulation capabilities for advanced aircraft and systems through the Test Pilots School's various Test Management Programs.

The VISTA is the premier in-flight simulation (IFS) vehicle for the latest manned and unmanned aircraft. IFS is the process of augmenting a 'host' aircraft, in this case VISTA, through a control system to simulate the handling characteristics and dynamics of another aircraft. Since the flight control system of the simulated aircraft is implemented in the host platform, its characteristics can be assessed in a real-world environment. Specific flight control system changes, flying qualities, architectures, failure modes, gain changes and control systems can all be evaluated.

The X-62A VISTA over Edwards Air Force Base, California. US Air Force/Kyle Brasier

Roger Tanner and Bill Gray piloted the NF-16D VISTA from Hill Air Force Base, Utah, to Edwards Air Force Base, California on January 30, 2019, after receiving modifications and a new paint scheme at the Ogden Air Logistics Complex. US Air Force/Christian Turner

VISTA'S ORIGINS

The initial concept originated in the mid-1970s when the US Air Force recognised the need for a replacement for the NT-33A IFS aircraft. Various design studies were conducted until the mid-1980s for the development of a full 6 Degree-Of-Freedom in-flight simulator. The purpose was to develop a full IFS capability for small, fighter-type aircraft using an airframe that had performance characteristics representative of modern fighters. The studies resulted in the selection of the F-16 for a 5 Degree-of-Freedom IFS (pitch, roll, yaw, lift and thrust). Production of the VISTA NF-16D was given to General Dynamics, Fort Worth Division, Texas in 1988 (now Lockheed Martin Aeronautics). Calspan Aerospace was selected to develop and integrate the aircraft's Variable Stability System (VSS) because of the company's expertise in flight control system development and IFS.

The N prefix given to the VISTA denoted its status as special test, permanent whose configuration is drastically changed that returning the aircraft to its original configuration or conversion to standard operational configuration is beyond practicable or economic limits.

CONFIGURATION

The resulting VISTA aircraft was a mixture of many different features, most of which were already available from previous F-16 production programmes. VISTA is a Block 30 F-16D (serial number 86-0048) airframe in Peace Marble II configuration, including a large dorsal fairing for installation of additional electronic equipment, and designated the NF-16D. The aircraft is fitted with the General Electric F110-GE-100B engine (with provisions

Block 42 F-16C 90-0726/WA loaded with two live 2,000lb GBU-10 laser-guided bombs departs runway 03L for a strike mission.

the air-to-air phase. To induce stress and get our students learning we have to ramp up the number of aircraft involved and the complexity of the sortie to a 4 v 8 or a 4 v 10".

WIC students do one full week of air-to-air sims prior to their live fly, and another five or so scattered throughout the course, each one to prepare them for a live fly mission. "Sims are great for building the foundation of what the student needs to execute, but there's nothing that compares to live flying for executing the mission. That's the focus of this course, and that's how they get the experience required," opined the 16th WPS spokesperson. *Mark Ayton*

Block 52 F-16D 91-0467/WA loaded with inert CATM-88 HARM missiles lands on runway 21L following a mission in the Suppression of Enemy Air Defences phase of the F-16 weapons instructor course.

F-16 Falcon Still in the Fight

There are various aggressor squadrons in the US Department of Defense. Three are in the US Air Force. Two fly the F-16C. One is based at Nellis Air Force Base, Nevada: the 64th Aggressor Squadron.

The aggressor programme began in the autumn of 1972 with the activation of the 64th Aggressor Squadron (AGRS). The unit was formed as a direct result of the high air combat loss rate experienced by the air force in the Vietnam War.

Operating a professional adversary force conducting a programme of intense dissimilar air combat training (DACT) was identified as the best means to reverse that trend. The new DACT replaced the traditional mock air-to-air engagements flown by pilots in the same type of aircraft at their home bases with aggressor pilots and controllers flying and employing tactics that emulated the former Soviet Union and other potential adversaries. Агрессоры is Russian for aggressors.

The 64th AGRS has flown the T-38 Talon and F-5E Tiger. Today it's equipped with about 30 of the oldest F-16Cs in the air force: a mix of Block 32 and Block 42s.

PLAYING MIG

The squadron's mission is to provide adversary support to the US Air Force Weapons School, Exercise Red Flag, and Green Flag, a large close air support training exercise. The aircraft are painted in different colour schemes, each designed to replicate

The Soviet red star is prominent in the 64th AGRS badge. Emile Schoonderwoerd

Block 42 F-16C 89-2048/WA painted in the all-black Wraith colour scheme recently adopted by the 64th AGRS. US Air Force/Senior Airman Zachary Rufus

fighters and the tactics of nations hostile to the United States. The 64th AGRS pilots play the roles of crews of fourth-generation MiG-29 Fulcrums, Su-27 Flankers, and fifth-generation Chinese J-20s to name a few.

A 64th AGRS spokesperson said: "There's no hiding that the jets are old. Most of them were built between 1985 and 1987. But they are holding up pretty good and have no problems in replicating other fourth-generation aircraft. We have no issues with the aircraft being able to manoeuvre like fourth-generation threat adversaries would in close air combat scenarios. It's still very capable and able to do that".

A spokesperson for the Nellis-based Adversary Tactics Support Squadron told the author: "The 64th, and aggressors at large, offer a depth of knowledge and the ability to replicate beyond just the set patterns that we write down on a piece of paper during briefings."

The aggressor role at Nellis is to train US and allied pilots in air-to-air combat by providing the most robust threat lay down in the world. That's tough to do considering the types of aircraft being replicated and their respective radar and air-to-air missile capabilities.

The decisions as to which aircraft and missile systems to replicate are driven by the desired learning objectives (DLO) issued by the Weapons School and the 414th Combat Training Squadron, the unit responsible for running Exercise Red Flag.

The 64th AGRS spokesperson explained: "If we're replicating an Su-27 or J-11B we adhere to limitations and characteristics in order to match their capabilities [radar system and missiles] versus the aircraft. So how do we know how to replicate those platforms and systems? By working with the intelligence agencies, which have representatives at Nellis who are experts in Chinese and Russian doctrine and weapon systems."

SUBJECT MATTER EXPERTS
The intent of the 64th AGRS is to hire instructor pilots. There was a time all pilots posted to the unit were instructors, selected for their experience and proficiency of mission employment, flight safety and training rules. That's not the case any more due to budget constraints and force reduction.

> "The 64th offer a depth of knowledge and the ability to replicate beyond just role patterns"
> Adversary Tactics Support Squadron

The 64th AGRS spokesperson was certain that the squadron's ability to conduct its mission has not been detracted, but he said the budget and force reduction had created a challenge in getting pilots trained to the appropriate level for the squadron's bread-and-butter work supporting Exercise Red Flag.

Whatever an individual's experience level, when they arrive at the 64th AGRS they start to work on qualifying as an aggressor wingman. Then they work towards becoming a lane lead, which enables them to lead up to an eight-ship.

With further training the pilot progresses to mission commander, which permits the officer to lead an entire package of aggressors. But that's not the top qualification. That's called MIG 1 and qualifies the individual to lead an entire Red Flag package which, depending on the number of assets and augmentees available, can comprise up to 30 aircraft.

"After you qualify as aggressor wingman, you work toward getting certified as a subject matter expert [SME]. We have SMEs in the flying squadron who are certified in aircraft, a good example is the Su-27 Flanker, while those assigned to the air defence squadron specialise in surface-to-air missile systems such as the SA-2 Guideline and SA-6 Gainful," said the spokesperson for the Adversary Tactics Support Squadron.

To achieve SME status the pilot takes an intensive course of study and reviews current information and intelligence data on Chinese and Russian systems, gathered by the intelligence agencies.

"The cross talk with the intel community is huge," affirmed the 64th AGRS spokesperson.

Each trainee must present an hour-long brief to a group of SMEs and squadron personnel. The SMEs ask many demanding questions to ascertain that the pilot has the depth of knowledge he requires.

"Once certified as an SME, we ask that pilot to go on the road as a member of our tactics analysis teams, who provide analysis and give briefings to the cast of Combat Air Force fighter units," explained the spokesperson for the Adversary Tactics Support Squadron.

Simulators are interspersed throughout flying training to introduce each new event and role. The initial academic elements can often seem overwhelming to the student because there's a lot of workbooks, classes and simulators before the student gets to sit in the jet. Students rely on civilian and military instructors who are well versed in how to make it make sense from the early stage.

In the first part, the student is introduced to the techniques required to take off, land, fly, and cruise. Instructor pilots (IPs) follow the student around the pattern and tell them to go around if they see something unsafe. Once a student pilot completes their check ride, they receive their initial Form 8, a certificate that shows they can safely pilot the aircraft in daytime visual and instrument conditions.

Students are then introduced to tactics starting with basic fighter manoeuvring, low aspect, followed by high aspect and then nose-to-nose BFM. These require a wider array of personal techniques, imparted to the students by different IPs.

Generally, pilots say the F-16 is not too hard to learn to fly, but it's hard to learn how to fight with when they try to use all the controls on the throttle and stick to make the jet do what they want: that's the challenge.

The air force uses a basic left hand-right hand instruction technique. An instructor pilot takes the student through the mission brief and instructs them at the start of the aerial battle to select max afterburner with their left hand, and with their right hand to roll out and fly to where the adversary starts their turn. When the student reaches that point, they must start their turn by pulling to 9G with their right hand and relax to freeze the adversary so they can start to decrease angles which will allow them to attack from a stable gunshot position.

That sequence happens in about five to seven seconds, so their left and right hands and their brain will not be moving as fast as they need to be. Because of the air combat manoeuvring instrumentation system used by the air force, the IP and the student can use the mission data recorded during the flight in the debrief. This enables the IP to identify when the student carried out their instructions.

The student may have selected max afterburner a little too late or pulled too hard when they needed to relax and apply back-stick pressure instead of pointing at the adversary.

During BFM, the tactical portion lasts for no more than 20 minutes but the debrief lasts about two hours. The 20-minute tactical portion in the first few BFM rides is a script. The student is likely to be soaked in sweat and breathing hard and will be barely hanging on by the end. The IP must get him to take a deep breath and prepare to return to Holloman and land just as they had learned to do in the transition phase.

Colonel Justin Spears, 49th Wing commander, after a flight from Homestead Air Reserve Base, Florida. US Air Force/Senior Airman Adrian Salazar

Four F-16s assigned to the 314th Fighter Squadron parked on the flightline at Homestead Air Reserve Base, Florida during Exercise Miami Agile Combat Employment, one of the first major detachments for a Holloman-based fighter squadron. US Air Force/Senior Airman Adrian Salazar

Students fly three offensive BFM flights and generally struggle with the first two, but on the third, nearly all students do better. Generally, students can keep up using the left hand-right hand mantra quite a bit more during the defensive BFM rides and most have figured things out by the end of the BFM phase.

AIR COMBAT MANOEUVRING

There are not many hours in the training programme so it is designed to cater for an average student such that if an individual gets to the end of the BFM phase the IPs can safely move them onto air combat manoeuvring (ACM). This primarily comprises 2 v 1 and 2 v 2 engagements, which means the student has a third and a fourth aircraft from which to de-conflict.

As with the start of the BFM phase, IPs find that the student's left and right hands and their brain are moving slower than required, so IPs must figure out where the lags are and speed up the student's execution.

The IPs try to make things as simple as they can for the students, so they have the brain capacity to keep up with what's going on. By primarily calling left hand, right hand, on the radio, the IP can get things to a simple state.

An IP can adapt each flight based on the student's ongoing performance. Some students perform well such that the IP can fly more aggressively against them – as if flying against another instructor. For students who are struggling, the IP keeps it simple and gets them to the minimum standard required by the air force.

TACTICAL INTERCEPTS

Following ACM, students move on to long-range tactical intercepts (TI) which trains them to use the radar to identify, target and shoot missiles to kill the adversary. Up until this point, the student has visually manoeuvred their aircraft in relation to another.

Students start with basic 1 v 1 long-range intercepts and then step-up to 2 v 2 and finally 4 v 4. In the complicated 4

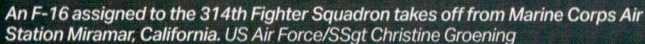
An F-16 assigned to the 314th Fighter Squadron takes off from Marine Corps Air Station Miramar, California. US Air Force/SSgt Christine Groening

v 4 scenarios IPs want the student to remain in formation and follow the flight lead around as they execute the tactics.

If the student can do that, it's nearly good enough. If the student can do that and take a shot or two, it's good. If the student can do that and shoot multiple contacts at the same time, they are doing well.

The TI phase culminates with a defensive counter air (DCA) mission in which the student is responsible for protecting a target. This is conducted in a simulator with multiple adversaries simulating a near-peer threat. During the mission, adversaries may fly at low-level to test the student to look down low as per the radar tactics instruction given to them.

Before the DCA mission, IPs spend a significant amount of time teaching academics and having informal one-on-one conversations with the students to ensure the student understands what's going to happen, their responsibilities, the importance of the sortie and the instructor's expectations.

In the air-to-air portion, which represents about half the training programme, the aircraft is configured in one of two ways. One configuration is referred to as a centreline bag jet fitted with just one fuel tank on the centreline (station 5). This configuration is used mostly for air-to-air training.

The configuration changes for the final portion of air-to-air training when the sorties are longer and require two fuel external tanks carried on under-wing stations 4 and 6; a configuration referred to as a two-bag jet.

BASIC SURFACE ATTACK AND PRECISION-GUIDED WEAPON EMPLOYMENT

Students conduct low-level step-down training to learn how to fly at 500ft and safely manoeuvre near the ground ahead of transitioning to the air-to-ground phase. The two-bag configuration is used throughout the air-to-ground phase.

When loaded with both laser and GPS-guided bombs, the student is presented with a lot of information, much of which isn't relevant, so the IPs try to encourage their brain into understanding what they must do to make the bomb hit the target.

IPs have extensive discussions with the student about what is considered a valid versus an invalid weapon employment. It's vital for the student to remember if they are dropping a GPS-guided weapon on a set of coordinates and accidentally bump a switch, they can induce a

A 314th Fighter Squadron F-16D taxis to the runway at Marine Corps Air Station Miramar, California on TDY. The 314th conducted dissimilar air combat training with jets assigned to Marine Fighter Attack Squadron 314 (VMFA-314). US Air Force/SSgt Christine Groening

Airmen from the 314th Aircraft Maintenance Unit ensure weapons are loaded to a 314th Fighter Squadron F-16C prior to a mission from Marine Corps Air Station Miramar, California. US Air Force/SSgt Christine Groening

slew into the system, leaving the jet thinking the target is not at the point given by the coordinates.

Students must follow in-depth DCLASSS laser checks. D reminds them to switch the DVR (tapes) on; C reminds them to place their Cursor to zero to remove any slew out of the system; L reminds them to check the Laser; A reminds them to check the jet's Altitude mode; S reminds them to chek the Stores Management System and the bomb; S reminds them to run a System check and make sure the GPS is accurate; and S reminds them to check the Steerpoint, to make sure the correct target coordinates are being used.

The checks ensure that the pilot has the right laser code. Different aircraft in a flight have different laser codes. Therefore, if the pilot laser-designates for one jet and then his own, but without resetting the laser coding for his jet, then the bomb will never detect the laser energy.

If a bomb malfunctions in combat and doesn't go where it's supposed to, the tapes will be checked to make sure the pilot applied the DCLASSS checks properly. If the pilot doesn't

F-16 Falcon Still in the Fight

Airmen from the 314th Aircraft Maintenance Unit conduct post-flight maintenance on an F-16 at Marine Corps Air Station Miramar, California. US Air Force/SSgt Christine Groening

F-16s from Luke Air Force Base, Arizona taxi toward the flight line after arriving at Holloman Air Force Base, New Mexico, on June 16, 2015. US Air Force/Airman 1st Class Emily Kenney

F-16 Falcon Still in the Fight

Two F-16s fly alongside a KC-135 Stratotanker assigned to the Ohio Air National Guard's 121st Air Refueling Wing based at Rickenbacker Air National Guard Base, Columbus, Ohio. US Air Force/Airman 1st Class Antonio Salfran

complete a proper check, they could miss or kill innocent people. IPs must ensure each student completes the course fully with the understanding that when they hit the pickle button, they are striking the right target.

Close air support (CAS), a primary role for the F-16, is introduced towards the end of the air-to-ground portion. Typically, the CAS missions are aligned with the final capstone Offensive Counter Air mission.

The student flies a strike mission as part of a four-ship that must fight adversaries on the way into the target area, find the proper target, conduct the DCLASSS check, drop the valid weapon and then fight adversaries on the way out. This is the capstone exercise of the B course and for a trainee multi-role fighter pilot.

MENTORING
Most pilots who qualify as instructors have the capability to mentor students. The difficulties of the job arise when a student has a few bad flights in a row.

In the syllabus, the student could do well on Monday and then be close to elimination from the programme by Thursday because of the permissible number of bust rides in place for non-progression.

An IP can be responsible for five pilots. Some of them may do well the whole time, others are up and down. IPs have closed-door discussions, which are off the record. An IP will relate to them by letting them know that they were once in the same shoes as the student and had a hard time. An IP will also get the student to realise that they are expected to make mistakes, that it is OK, and they must compartmentalise their errors.

There is nothing the student can do because the mistake is done and the individual must move on, either to the rest of the flight if they have made a mistake during a flight or to the next flight. An IP must always try to instil the ability to accept their mistake, move on and get back to a positive attitude.

MISSION QUALIFICATION TRAINING
Before the course half-way point the 314th FS co-ordinates with the 54th Fighter Group's personnel centre to determine the operational assignments for student pilots.

The basic course is followed by a further six weeks' training covering Block-specific avionic and mission systems. This is important for each pilot transferring to a Combat Air Force unit operating a specific Block of aircraft, all of which have different configurations. Once a new pilot arrives at their operational unit, they spend up to 90 days completing initial mission qualification training (MQT). Completion of MQT qualifies them to deploy with their squadron and conduct combat tasking as a wingman.

SYLLABUS RELEVANCE
The B course syllabus is reviewed on an annual basis and small changes around the fringes are made.

The 54th Fighter Group refers to Air Combat Command and the other major commands to tell them what's required in the syllabus. Air Education and Training command then changes the syllabus to meet the requirements.

That said, the syllabus is extremely robust. The most significant addition in recent years was precision-guided weapon delivery and the provision of more rounds for practising strafing and a close air support component.

Furthermore, the 54th FG places a new emphasis on near peer adversary aircraft and surface-to-air weapons systems in order to address the United States' pacing threat.

ZIA SUN
Exercise Zia Sun is a routine close air support exercise hosted by the 3rd Air Support Operations Group from Fort Hood, Texas. Joint training involves Tactical Air Control Parties

F-16C 88-0464/HO assigned to the 314th Fighter Squadron taxis to the runway at Tyndall Air Force Base, Florida, on March 8, 2021. The aircraft was taking part in Combat Archer, a Weapons System Evaluation Program dedicated to launching air-to-air missiles. US Air Force/Airman 1st Class Tiffany Price

An F-16 from the 314th Fighter Squadron aerial refuelling from a KC-135 Stratotanker over New Mexico on November 15, 2022. US Air Force/Airman 1st Class Nicholas Paczkowski

and Joint Terminal Attack Controllers working with different types of aircraft, typically A-10s, AC-130s, F-16s and MQ-9s. Hosted annually, it provides student F-16 pilots based at Holloman an opportunity to train with instructors in challenging and complex large-scale combat scenarios. Though the exercise is not part of the B course it does enable students to complete their syllabus learning objectives.

Missions flown over the Centennial range complex in New Mexico involve real-time close air support which adds to the reality of the scenarios for both the TACPs, JTACs and pilots.

During a recent edition, Holloman-based F-16 squadrons provided close air support each day. Tasking in the first week involved striking specific targets with inert munitions and in the second week convoy escort and searching for opposing forces.

Lt Col Sanford said: "We usually participate when the student's phase of training aligns with close air support, and we involve our instructor pilots because there is a significant amount of coordination and expertise required to effectively manage the scenarios. The driving force behind staging Exercise Zia Sun is being able to integrate joint and multinational forces in a complex scenario with weapons and personnel in close proximity. This aligns our lines of effort and ensures if needed, we can integrate multiple aircraft, ground systems and hundreds of personnel to effectively gain and maintain air and ground superiority."

AGILE COMBAT EMPLOYMENT

On June 23, 2022, the US Air Force announced its vision for operating in modern, contested environments created to codify and synchronise agile combat employment (ACE) tactics enterprise wide.

In the news release, the US Air Force stated: "Adversary threats to US Air Force operations at forward bases can deny US power projection, overwhelm traditional defence designs, impose prohibitive losses and lead to joint mission failure. To address these challenges, ACE shifts operations from centralized physical infrastructures to a network of smaller, dispersed locations or cluster bases."

US Air Force Chief of Staff General CQ Brown made it clear: "Fundamentally changing the way we generate airpower will complicate adversary planning and provide more options for our joint force and coalition commanders. Our approach to operations over the past 20 years has prioritised efficiency in an environment that is not highly contested. ACE puts the premium on effectiveness in an increasingly challenging threat environment."

Operationalising ACE will aid in: the codification of a repeatable and understandable process; forces that are suitably organized, trained, and equipped; theatres of operation that are postured with the appropriate equipment, assets and host nation agreements; and robust joint service and partner nation integration and interoperability.

At the tactical level, the ACE approaches and capabilities must enable dispersed forces to adapt and prevail despite uncertainty, using the best information available to local commanders. This will necessitate shifting between offensive and defensive operations in response to what is achievable with available connectivity and logistical support.

At the operational level for centralised command and distributed control, understanding what forces can achieve with available resources and trade-off risks becomes critical. Offensive and defensive capabilities and expertise available at each forward operating location may vary, as will available logistical support.

The ACE framework provides the USAF the ability to develop, maintain, and share timely, accurate, and relevant mission information across dispersed forces despite adversary attempts to deny or degrade it. It also prepares leaders to make and disseminate risk-informed decisions with limited information.

General Brown said: "Adapting to this new paradigm shift ensures we maintain a combat-effective force. Our airmen can expect to conduct operations at a speed, scope, complexity, and scale exceeding recent campaigns from distributed locations with increased survivability and enhanced effectiveness."

Those whose jobs are more directly connected to operations in general, and ACE in particular, will require more focused training on how to be multi-capable on an airfield. The exact breakout of Air Force Specialty Codes and required skills are being determined.

The intent is to train airmen to be more productive on discrete, wartime tasks that would reduce the number of airmen in harm's way in austere environments.

The US Air Force is implementing and evolving its agile combat employment (ACE) concept of operations across all combat-coded units and is starting to impact on how student pilots are trained.

Explaining the impact, Lt Col Sanford said his goal is to ensure students are best prepared for their first fighter squadron. "But because the air force is starting to move away from the big base concept towards one suited to a near peer threat, my goal for now is to sprinkle ACE into suitable TDY deployments as an introduction for the students and get them outside of their comfort zone. We can achieve that by operating from a different location and train without the standard support setups."

MIAMI ACE

In February, the 314th deployed to Homestead Air Reserve Base, Florida for an exercise called Miami Agile Combat Employment. Over 200 airmen generated off-station F-16 flight operations. This was the first time for many of them, and the first time the 54th FG had integrated ACE into the Fighter Training Unit construct at Holloman Air Force Base since the inception of the 54th FG.

In a news release issued on March 13, 2023, Lt Col Sanford said: "The biggest challenge we needed to overcome was comfort.

We needed to learn how to operate outside our comfort zone and with fewer resources and prove we can operate with less equipment."

Meeting the challenges throughout the exercise resulted in airmen acquiring the ability to serve in other specialties. This included pilots becoming qualified to re-fuel and prep their aircraft without maintainer support and training integration with other diverse aircraft.

Major Corbin Boyles, 314th FS Miami ACE project officer said: "We were programmed to accomplish more sorties, upgrades, and syllabus events than on any previous deployment and did so without sacrificing our fighter training unit timeline. The airspace allowed us to build more realistic training scenarios due to its accessibility and involvement of other aircraft platforms. This gave us the ability to work on our cross-platform tactics."

Sixteen F-16 aircraft were involved with a selection of student and instructor pilots. As part of the training afforded, Lt Col Sanford gave them the opportunity to learn how to refuel their own aircraft at an austere base. He said: "Aircrew don't usually refuel aircraft because it's undertaken by fuel specialists so the opportunity to do so safely was a means to improve their ability to operate in austere environments. After completing a tactical training mission, the pilots undertook aerial refuelling, then landed at Naval Air Station Key West, completed the refuel under the supervision by two multi capable airmen and two other maintainers who had arrived beforehand. They showed the pilots how to use the refuelling equipment. Not an easy task to complete and one that required the pilots to be careful in how they did it, but the objectives were successfully met. Then the aircraft took off, flew another mission, and landed back at Homestead.

Lt Colonel Sanford said: "Funding for the deployment was allocated, and Air Education and Training Command tasked the 314th to deploy to a different base to develop the skill set of the airmen involved and to incorporate some aspects of the ACE concept at a basic level. The idea was to better prepare the students for when they leave Holloman for their first combat-coded squadron. Homestead was selected because of the nearby available airspace and the opportunity to integrate jointly with F-22s, F-35s and US Navy jets."

Commenting on the success of the Miami ACE exercise, Lt Col Sanford said: "The 314th was scheduled to fly 200 sorties. We flew 205 because our maintenance component and airmen were able to maintain the aircraft at a very high reliability rate while deployed. Because of the weather and the available airspace, we were able to create incredible training opportunities, and introduce a few ACE events. But the real impact was the fourth- and fifth-generation integration.

"For the students involved, flying from Holloman to Homestead was the first time in their career they had flown for that long in an F-16 and the first time they had to land at a different base, which is a challenge. As a fighter pilot, one of the most rewarding things is to do something new and different and learn from it. All the pilots involved got that, it was great training value."

ONGOING ACE TRAINING

Completing an exercise like Miami ACE is a means to integrate basic aspects of the ACE concept safely and smoothly into fighter pilot training and is certainly a way to do so before the methods are formalised by the US Air Force.

The current B course executed by the three F-16 squadrons in the 54th Fighter Group follows a traditional concept of operations in which F-16s take off from Holloman, fly their missions, and recover to Holloman. That flight routine is followed throughout all phases of the seven-and-a-bit month syllabus because that's what the students need. But this flight routine is completely aligned with the big base concept. One question put to Lt Col Sanford was whether Air Education and Training Command needs to prepare students towards the end of the B course in practising some dispersed operations around an area as they will have to practice once they get to a combat-coded squadron? "Taking off from Holloman, completing the mission and then returning to Holloman is very important to create safe and effective fighter pilots in accordance with the current syllabus, and we still have to focus on that," he said. "But at the same time, we must look outside the box and listen to the ideas that our newer instructor pilots and joint partners have and to see if we can integrate them.

"Those are baby steps that we can do unit by unit, but eventually we'll follow orders to ensure we're training student pilots who can meet the objectives of agile combat employment. Before the air force writes the syllabus to include such changes, it falls to commanders and airmen to do it safely at the unit level. We must continue to use innovative ways to build combat airpower in the future and can't wait on somebody else to tell us how to do it. That said, my number one responsibility is to safely get students through the syllabus."

QUICK TURN CONSTRUCT

Last year the 314th's director of operations and the maintenance unit created a sortie generation model that enables jets to be turned quicker and safer by also integrating with the 311th FS which shares ramp space with the 314th FS.

Explaining, Lt Col Sanford said: "The director of operations was able to create a construct which allowed us to utilise the other squadron's planes, and they utilise our planes. As a result, we can turn jets quicker and more efficiently. Consequently, the 314th FS flew the most sorties and hours of any fighter squadron at Holloman in 2022.

"It compressed time between arrival and departure and allowed the flying window to be shortened. When the flying window is shortened, the jet can be worked on for longer. Now the other squadrons are running with the construct to improve the flow process. Use of the construct really allowed us to step ahead as far as how much we're able to fly and kept us a little bit ahead of the pack as far as how many students we can produce as well."

Back in late 2019, the 49th Wing's flagship F-16 was 88-0412 which was painted with this colourful tail. US Air Force/SSgt Christine Groening

F-16D 90-0788/HO assigned to the 314th Fighter Squadron takes off from Tyndall Air Force Base, Florida, for a Combat Archer Weapons System Evaluation Program mission. US Air Force/Airman 1st Class Tiffany Price

F-16 Falcon Still in the Fight

Florida Makos

Mark Ayton spoke with Lieutenant Colonel David Sproehnle, commander of the 93rd Fighter Squadron based at Homestead Air Reserve Base, Florida.

The 93rd Fighter Squadron's flag ship, F-16C 88-0405/FM seen on take-off from Homestead Air Reserve Base. US Air Force/Captain Michael Balserak

F-16 Falcon Still in the Fight

The 93rd Fighter Squadron – nicknamed the Makos - is a combat-coded squadron in Air Force Reserve Command with the same mission set as other F-16 units across the US Air Force, except for suppression of enemy air defence. The squadron flies and fights alongside active-duty units with one difference - a good number of the airwomen and airmen assigned are not full time.

The squadron's commander is Lieutenant Colonel David Sproehnle, an F-16 pilot with a career that includes B-52, MQ-1, RQ-170, and T-38. Describing some of the squadron's flight operations he said: "We fly big mouth Block 30 F-16Cs [powered by GE Aerospace F110 engines], we fly up to 18 sorties per day, we've got airspace around the Florida peninsula and follow a phase-based training programme involving air-to-air, air-to-ground, and close air support, and continually rotate through them. The only specific mission we hold is to sit alert for the defence of the United States as a backup to the Florida Air National Guard's alert mission, which we do occasionally, but not throughout the year."

TASKINGS

Squadron taskings come from the Secretary of the Air Force through the Chief of Staff of the Air Force and then from Headquarters, Air Force Reserve Command.

Explaining how day-to-day flight operations are determined and funded Lt Col Sproehnle said the squadron is given an annual flying hours programme to manage and the money to pay for all flying.

He said: "Each pilot has a minimum number of sorties they are expected to fly each month based on their experience level. We submit a request for the number of hours we expect to fly in any given year. The submission goes for approval by Air Force Reserve Command and then HQ, US Air Force. The budget as awarded is then managed by the 10th Air Force based at Fort Worth, Texas and is updated quarterly. Fort Worth is where the reserve component's Numbered Air Force is commanded."

Each quarter, the squadron declares how many hours it flew and how many it had expected to fly. Any hours not flown in that quarter are given back to 10th Air Force for redistribution to other units that may be flying more, or vice versa. Similarly, if the squadron has over flown, and another unit has under flown, 10th Air Force will reflow some money back.

Lt Col Sproehnle said: "The 93rd FS is still the largest TFI squadron in the entire US Air Force. We currently have ten active-duty pilots flying with us for which ACC provides funding to cover the cost of the additional flying hours flown by the active-duty pilots. In terms of a flight schedule, we combine all requirements and create the flight schedule required to ensure all pilots get the required sorties.

"Active duty, Air National Guard and Reserve units are pretty much standard with few differences. However, the number of sorties and the number simulators required each month does differ. That's because reserve squadrons typically have a greater level of experience among their pilot cadre.

"Typically, our experienced reserve pilots fly one or two fewer sorties per month than our less experienced reserve and active-duty pilots who fly a specific number of sorties per month to make sure they are gaining the

A load crew loads a 2,000lb-class bomb onto an F-16C during the 482nd Aircraft Maintenance Squadron's quarterly load crew competition at Homestead Air Reserve Base. Load crews were evaluated in four areas to determine the winner: dress and personal appearance, tool kit inspection, a general knowledge test, and actual munitions loading to include speed and proficiency. US Air Force/TSgt Leo Castellano

experience required to get comfortable with the aircraft. We need about 4,000 sorties per year, minimum, to meet our aircrew requirements. That's around 5,600 hours or so.

"This year's programme [2023] is just under 3,000 sorties, and 4,300 hours. because our jets have been going through upgrade we've not had as many here, so we've been operating on a reduced flying schedule for almost two years, so the amount of experience gained by the active-duty component on the 93rd FS during that timeframe has dropped. As more aircraft return from the upgrade programme the numbers should go back up.

"The point of the TFI [Total Force Integration] programme is to allow junior pilots from across the entire fleet to be absorbed into flying jobs when the active duty doesn't have enough aircraft for all of them, so the air force assigns them to Air National Guard and Reserve squadrons to get experience. Furthermore, we've got a cadre of experienced pilots and instructors, some with over 1,000 hours, that can teach them and get them upgraded to flight leads or potentially even instructor pilots, after which they return to the active-duty force. That's the goal."

PHASED-BASED TRAINING

Discussing the phase-based training programme, Lt Col Sproehnle said the squadron starts with the basics of every mission set: "For example, when we're going through an air-to-air phase, we'll start off with basic fighter manoeuvres [BFM], flying 1 v 1, simulating whatever threat we're replicating at the time. Then we'll move on to air combat manoeuvring [ACM] with multiple blue air aircraft versus one red air aircraft, in which we work as a team to take out a single threat. Then move into tactical intercepts which involves finding a target at long-range and intercepting that target in a position of advantage. We then usually move into defensive counter air, protecting a point with a four-ship of F-16s against as many red air jets that we can push.

"After that we usually move into basic surface attack starting at the bombing range flying rectangular patterns, dropping bombs to get used to the sight pictures and the procedures for rolling in from different angles, different altitudes, and precision bomb dropping. Then we move to the surface attack phase. We fight our way in against surface-to-air missiles and other ground threats, mostly to drop bombs in a more dynamic environment. From there, we'll move into close air support training. Ground units deploy to the Avon Park range just south of Orlando who provide us with tactical air control against targets of interest.

"Then we top it all off with the opposed surface attack, our bread-and-butter tasking with a standard fighting element of four F-16s against any number of red air jets with the intent

Airmen assigned to the 482nd Aircraft Maintenance Squadron load inert AIM-120 AMRAAM air-to-air missiles on an F-16 during an Operational Readiness Inspection. US Air Force/Tim Norton

PHASE MAINTENANCE

F-16s, like all US Air Force aircraft, undergo two types of maintenance at their home station – scheduled and phase. Aircraft maintenance squadrons perform scheduled maintenance, and the phase flight conducts the deeper tear-down phase maintenance.

Phase is the most detailed maintenance carried out by the 482nd Maintenance Group. The F-16 undergoes a 400-, 800- (taking five days) and a 2,400-hour phase (lasting nine days).

For phase, maintainers open all the panels and inspect areas in accordance with work cards and applicable technical data. They get behind components, look carefully at the wires to make sure there's no chafing and inspect inside the aircraft, looking for cracks and gouges on bulkheads. If they find either they seek advice from engineers at the depot to determine if they are allowed to carry out repairs or if they need a depot team to undertake repair for them.

At the start of each fiscal Year the maintenance group designs a phase flow that shows when individual aircraft must enter phase throughout the 12 months. Flow is based on the year's projected flying hours and the number of airmen available. It is monitored and adjusted on a weekly basis. The maintenance group can adjust which aircraft is coming in for phase. If a specific aircraft is flying more regularly or an aircraft is down for maintenance and is not accruing its normal flight hours, it gets pushed back in the phase flow and another aircraft is moved forward.

On the first day in phase maintainers look for damage that can be repaired quickly and what parts need to be ordered. They are very specific on what parts can be ordered and how they are sourcing the equipment. Is it cheaper or better for them to cannibalise another aircraft, or is it worth waiting for the part to come in? Having a detailed look through the records saves them a lot of time because the required parts should be ordered and delivered by the time the maintainers need them.

The maintenance group tries to bundle as much maintenance as possible into X number of days and share resources every week. That means other shops come into phase to carry out maintenance at the same time, provided it does not interfere with the phase process. Examples are inspections of the canopy, seat, and the engine.

Associated components, such as pylons, bomb racks and missile rails, are removed depending on how long the aircraft will be in phase. Such components are scheduled to their own time cycle inspections.

Engines are removed and serviced based on the aircraft's phase cycle, when the engine's next inspection is due and when broken components are found in the engine bay.

Condensation streams over the wings of a 93rd Fighter Squadron F-16C during an aerial demonstration at the Homestead Air Reserve Base air show. US Air Force/93rd Fighter Squadron/Barrera Photography

of bombing a target. We fight our way in, drop bombs, fight our way out, and return home. That's the culmination of our mission set. Then we start back over with the BFM phase again."

EXERCISES AT HOMESTEAD

Prior to the COVID pandemic, the 482nd Fighter Wing held a regular large force exercise, called CHUMEX, bringing together multiple units and aircraft for training focused on teamwork and real-world combat scenarios. The COVID lockdown prevented further iterations. In February 2023, the 482nd Fighter Wing staged an Exercise called Miami Agile Combat Employment, the first attempt to host a large force exercise post-COVID.

Homestead Air Reserve Base is well suited to host such an event with a huge ramp to park visiting aircraft and lots of airspace suitable for both air-to-air and air-to-ground training. There are more than adequate facilities for hosting different types of aircraft to undertake fourth and fifth generation integration.

During the exercise the 93rd FS worked with F-22 Raptors assigned to the 27th FS from Langley, 314th FS F-16s from Holloman, 60th FS F-35A Lighting IIs from Eglin, and multiple US Navy assets.

Given Homestead's location at the tip of the Florida peninsula, geographically its distance from other fighter bases in northern Florida means the 93rd FS faces challenges to organise air-to-air training with dissimilar types of fighter aircraft. Most air-to-air training involves blue and red air sections of its own jets or US Navy and US Marine Corps F/A-18s operating from Naval Air Station Key West. Commenting on the situation, Lt Col Sproehnle said: "Ideally, we'd love to get different types here at Homestead that we don't see that often. We fight with the US Navy F-5 aggressors based at Key West as much as possible, though they don't have a tonne of gas which is a limiting factor as to where and how long they can fight. We also arrange air-to-air training with the Florida Air National Guard F-15C Eagles based at Jacksonville in the northeast of the state."

Typically, the 93rd FS tries to participate in a couple of large force exercises per year in preparation for a deployment, though the COVID pandemic adjusted that. In recent years, the 93rd FS participated in Sentry Savannah hosted by the Combat Readiness Training Center at Savannah IAP, Sentry Aloha at Hickam Air Base, Hawaii, and Exercise Iniohos at Andravida Air Base, Greece. This year the unit deployed to Tyndall Air Force Base in May for Exercise Checkered Flag.

In early June 2021, the 93rd FS returned from a combat tour in Afghanistan. Along with the New Jersey Air National Guard's F-16C-equipped 119th Fighter Squadron, they were the last fighter squadrons deployed in country leading up to the withdrawal by US forces completed in August 2021.

The deployment to Bagram Air Base started in December 2020 and was extended for over a month. The 119th Fighter Squadron joined the 93rd FS mid-deployment but moved its operations out of country and continued to cover the vuls from another base in the CENTCOM theatre. The 93rd FS aircraft left Bagram on the same day the last combat

F-16C 86-0266/FM assigned to the 93rd Expeditionary Fighter Squadron over a breath-taking backdrop of snow-covered mountains in Afghanistan. The aircraft is loaded with live weapons: an AIM-120 AMRAAM air-to-air missile and 500lb GBU-38 JDAMs. US Air Force/Captain Michael Balserak

sorties were flown from the base. During its combat tour, the 93rd FS dropped two types of Joint Direct Attack Munitions: 500lb GBU-38s, 500lb GBU-54 Laser Joint Direct Attack Munitions, and 250lb GBU-39 Small Diameter Bombs. Additionally, the squadron employed AGR-20 rockets and 20mm rounds fired from the M61A1 Vulcan cannon. The squadron conducted 24/7 ops conducting sorties with four to six hours average duration including at least three aerial refuellings per sortie.

Lt Col Sproehnle said: "The CFACC [combined force air component commander] at the time praised us and said it was the best fighter operation he'd seen during his time in the desert. So those accolades carried high with us that we were able to meet all our sortie production. All our employments were within the requirements and got the job done. We had exceeded his expectations."

Summing up, Lt Col Sproehnle highlighted the strategic location of Homestead Air Reserve Base which is surrounded by some of the greatest airspace in the world, which allows for the next generation of training in which fifth-generation fighters can employ. He said: "We are in regular conversations about what's going to happen to the base and to the unit here. Obviously, we're hoping another fighter jet will recapitalise the Makos. Put simply, there is two miles of concrete out here that's being underutilised."

AIRCRAFT MAINTENANCE SQUADRON

The fighter squadron is supported by an Aircraft Maintenance Squadron or AMS which has a Weapons Flight (Armament), Tactical Aircraft Maintenance Specialist Flight (crew chiefs) and a Specialist Flight (electronic environmental, avionics and propulsion troops) assigned, all of which work on the flight line.

A Production Flight has the expeditors and production superintendents, who direct the three main flights listed above, and a fifth support section is responsible for aircraft ground equipment, tools, and tech data.

The AMS' number one objective is to support the weekly flight schedule.

The production team and the fighter squadron set each week's flight schedule. The extent of the flight schedule accounts for aircraft availability and the AMS' manning.

Crew chiefs, avionics and weapons airmen arrive at work during the early part of the morning to check the servicing and prepare the aircraft. They launch the aircraft for the first go and react to any system malfunction or discrepancy that occurs once the pilot is in the aircraft, known as 'red ball maintenance', by either fixing the problem on the spot or after shutdown and ground abort.

Any discrepancies reported by the pilots after the mission are fixed in a three-hour turn window, which also requires refuelling and reloading if munitions are required.

The day shift also checks the servicing and conducts thorough inspections to prepare the aircraft for the second go. The swing shift catch the aircraft after the second mission and undertake the maintenance, repairs, and pre-flight inspections ready for the next day's flying.

A salvo of flares falls to the ground behind the dispensing F-16C during an aerial demonstration at the Homestead Air Reserve Base air show. US Air Force/93rd Fighter Squadron/Barrera Photography

BACK SHOPS

The Propulsion Flight can completely strip down an engine and rebuild the powerplant, its back shop does all F110 engine phase maintenance. The engine overhaul process requires the maintainers to de-case the entire engine, take the turbine wheel and all the bearings off and tear it down to its base elements. All components removed are then overhauled by different sections. If all the parts required are available, an overhaul takes up to 15 days to complete.

The Avionics Flight services the digital flight control system, throttle sticks, control sticks, switches, head-up displays, radars, radar dishes, avionics, navigational and radio equipment. The Avionics Flight runs bench tests to validate the component's serviceability status. If broken, the component may be repaired in house but in most cases, it is returned to the depot.

The Accessories Flight has different sections all geared to phase maintenance. The Electrical and Environmental section works the electrical environmental components. This involves back shop repair of lighting control panels, lighting systems, servicing the oxygen bailout bottles for pilots, servicing liquid oxygen and nitrogen carts used for servicing aircraft, and generator systems.

The Fuel Systems section maintains aircraft fuel systems, tanks, pumps, transfer systems, external fuel tanks and air refuelling systems. Every aircraft that enters phase maintenance goes to the fuel cell first for preventative maintenance, fuel system leaks and component failures.

The Egress Systems section inspects and services ejection seats, canopies, time change items, and strictly time-limited explosive items. Ejection seats are usually removed if something is lost in the crew station or if a component located underneath the seat needs servicing.

F-16C aircraft assigned to the 93rd Expeditionary Fighter Squadron parked on a hardened dispersal area at Bagram Air Base, Afghanistan. *US Air Force/Captain Michael Balserak*

The pilot of an F-16C aircraft assigned to the 93rd Expeditionary Fighter Squadron in the pre-contact position prior to aerial refuelling with a KC-10A Extender over Afghanistan. US Air Force/Captain Michael Balserak

This shot of an F-16C shows the aerial refuelling probe of the KC-10A Extender reflected in the aircraft's canopy in the early evening light of Afghanistan. US Air Force/Captain Michael Balserak

CREW CHIEF

Ever seen an F-16 being prepared for launch and wondered who the person is working on the jet while the pilot runs through the ground and pre-flight checks? That's the crew chief, and he or she is responsible for the safety of the aircraft.

Everything the crew chief does is a pre-flight check for the pilot. They make sure the inspections and scheduled maintenance are up to date.

Prior to the pilot stepping to the jet the crew chief checks for hydraulic fluid and oil leaks, as well as foreign object debris inside the intake. They also ensure the crew station is safe by checking switches, the ejection seat, and the oxygen bottle.

Once the checks and inspection are complete the crew chief signs a form to confirm they have been undertaken. For the period the aircraft is in the air, the crew chief is the airman who said this plane is good to fly.

After engine start, the crew chief verifies functionality of the flight control surfaces and the brakes. While the pilot moves the flight controls around, the crew chief visually checks roll left, roll right, rudder left, rudder right, rudder centre, nose up and nose down. When the pilot activates the brakes, the crew chief watches the pumps move and makes sure there are no hydraulic fluid leaks. Leaks are a common cause of a ground abort.

The crew chief also checks the Emergency Power Unit indicator, the engine start system and the pressure indicators which are known as delta Ps. Once the jet is pressurised, if a filter is contaminated a small, bright red indicator pops down. That means the aircraft must be shut down. The filter must be removed and inspected for contamination although the alert can often be caused by a bad delta P, because they expire over time.

There are three things a crew chief must be aware of for his or her personal safety while the aircraft is running - the noise, being ingested into the engine and getting in the way of the exhaust. The flight control surfaces also present a danger. If the pilot taps the side stick while moving around in the cockpit, just a slight nudge will cause the fly-by-wire system to move the surfaces and potentially hit the crew chief if he, or she, is in the way.

Once the pre-flight checks are complete the crew chief tells the pilot who will then clear them off the aircraft. First the crew chief disconnects the comm cord and shuts its door. They then lay the comm cord off to the side, pull the right-side chocks out and move them clear of the aircraft. Then they walk underneath the exhaust and pull the left side chocks from under the aircraft and move to the front of the aircraft in a position that will place them out of the exhaust when the jet turns. Finally, they direct the aircraft out.

On recovery the crew chief makes sure the aircraft is safe by checking the EPUs, hydraulics, and that the pins are fitted before shutdown. The peak time for fixing a write-up is when the engine is turning so the crew chief will keep the pilot there as long as they can, to fix the problem in chocks. If they can't fix it there, they'll shut the jet down and work on it later.

F-16 Falcon Still in the Fight

An atmospheric night-time shot of a 93rd Expeditionary Fighter Squadron F-16C on a hardened dispersal area at Bagram Air Base, Afghanistan while undergoing an engine change. Note the red guard on the inlet and the rocket pod loaded on the underwing weapon station. US Air Force/Captain Michael Balserak

F-16C 87-0239/FM loaded with inert AIM-120 AMRAAM air-to-air missiles and 500lb bombs shown on take-off from Homestead Air Reserve Base. *US Air Force/Captain Michael Balserak*

Mile High Militia

140th Wing/US Air National Guard

A grey overcast day greeted the 120th Fighter Squadron on its homecoming to Buckley Air Force Base, near Aurora, Colorado on May 15. Twelve F-16Cs touched down on the gigantic 11,000ft runway following a transpacific flight from Kunsan Air Base in South Korea. The 120th Expeditionary Fighter Squadron was at the Korean superbase on a 90-day Theater Security Package deployment. This was the eighth deployment made by the unit since September 11, 2001.

Lt Col Mitchell Neff, the 120th Expeditionary Fighter Squadron (EFS) commander said the unit flew air interdiction and close air support missions with the resident F-16C-equipped 35th and 80th Fighter Squadrons. Both are assigned to Pacific Air Forces' 8th Fighter Wing 'Wolf Pack'. The Colorado Guardsmen also flew with the Republic of Korea Air Force (RoKAF) 38th Fighter Group's 111th Fighter Squadron in three large force exercises.

Such deployments are an integral part of US Pacific Command's posture for averting threats to regional security and stability.

> Written in 2015, some of the technical aspects discussed within this chapter have been superseded or now come to fruition.

A Colorado Guardsman refuels an F-16C during Exercise Eager Lion in Jordan. SMSgt John Rohrer/US Air National Guard

A 140th Maintenance Squadron crew chief prepares an F-16 for take-off as part of a scramble competition event between the Colorado Air National Guard and the Royal Jordanian Air Force during Exercise Eager Lion. SMSgt John Rohrer/US Air National Guard

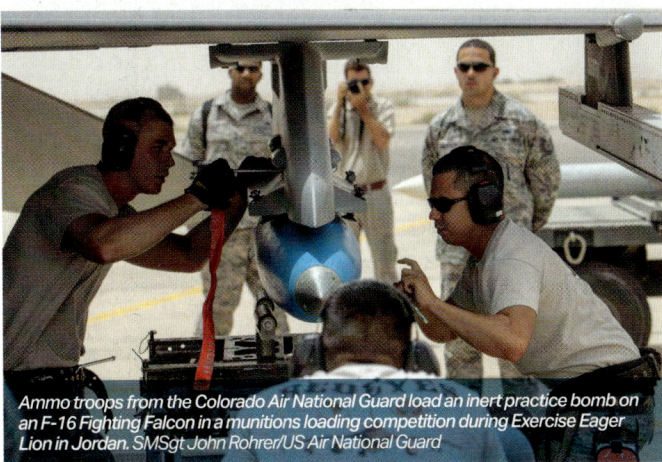
Ammo troops from the Colorado Air National Guard load an inert practice bomb on an F-16 Fighting Falcon in a munitions loading competition during Exercise Eager Lion in Jordan. SMSgt John Rohrer/US Air National Guard

A pilot performs a pre-flight inspection on an F-16 Fighting Falcon before a training mission during Exercise Red Flag, at Nellis Air Force Base, Nevada. TSgt Wolfram Stumpf/US Air National Guard

The intake cover is rolled up by a crew chief during the pre-flight of an F-16 for a mission from Nellis Air Force Base during Exercise Red Flag. TSgt Wolfram Stumpf/US Air National Guard

A 120th Fighter Squadron pilot shares a laugh with his crew chief before starting pre-flight checks. TSgt Wolfram Stumpf/US Air National Guard

A crew chief assigned to the 140th Maintenance Squadron relays information to the pilot during final aircraft checks at Red Flag. TSgt Wolfram Stumpf/US Air National Guard

Colorado Air National Guard ammo troops handle an inert practice bomb during Exercise Eager Lion in Jordan. SMSgt John Rohrer/US Air National Guard

F-16 Falcon Still in the Fight

"The F-16 is a jack of all trades and a master of none, but it's one of the most valuable platforms in our arsenal because it's got a lot of flexibility"

Lt Col Scott Vanbeek, Commander of the 140th Operational Support Squadron

As the pilot taxies out for a mission at Nellis Air Force Base a crew chief gives a salute. TSgt Wolfram Stumpf/US Air National Guard

Kunsan is the only base in the Republic of Korea that houses US and RoKAF flying squadrons. For the 120th EFS, the mix of force elements provided opportunities for combined bilateral training.

Lt Col Neff said: "We've been able to integrate with the 8th Fighter Wing in its operational readiness exercises and through a transparent mission planning process understand how we would take part in combat operations."

Before deploying to Kunsan, the squadron undertook night and electronic attack training, and three pilots completed instructor upgrades.

REDEYES

The 120th Fighter Squadron (FS) 'Redeyes' is assigned to Colorado Air National Guard's 140th Wing based at Buckley. It is equipped with 24 Block 32 F-16C Fighting Falcons.

Buckley is located 22 miles (35km) to the southeast of Denver, which is billed as the 'Mile High City': a reference to its altitude above sea level and the basis for the 120th's 'Mile High Militia' nickname.

The Wing started its transition from the A-7D Corsair II in 1992 when the first F-16 arrived. Like many US Air National Guard F-16 wings, the 140th is a multi-role unit as Lt Col Scott Vanbeek, the 140th Operational Support Squadron's commander explained: "We have typically been tasked with the close air support mission on our most recent deployments, but also train for the defensive and offensive counter air, and air interdiction roles."

Thanks to tremendous support from Colorado's senators and state legislators, the wing was successful in procuring AAQ-28 Litening targeting pods and Situation Awareness Data Link (SADL) sets. Lt Col Vanbeek said: "Both systems have made us extremely relevant in today's CAS [close air support] environment in Iraq. We have the ability to see things on the ground because of the targeting pod, and thanks to SADL we are also able to connect to Link 16 [within the battle space] to find out what's happening on the ground."

The Raytheon SADL connects the aircraft with a ground unit via the US Army's Enhanced Position Location Reporting System (EPLRS) on a robust, secure and jam-resistant data communication link. Operating in the air-to-ground mode, a pilot can command the SADL radio to synchronise with a specific ground network. The radio shares data between aircraft while recording ground positions from the EPLRS network. The SADL radio is integrated with the aircraft's avionics via a MIL-1553-STD data bus, providing the pilot with data from other SADL-equipped aircraft as well as the

Mile High Militia

positions of EPLRS-equipped aircraft and ground units.

"We thought outside the box," said Lt Col Vanbeek, "we knew the army was using the SADL radios in their Humvee vehicles, and determined [that] we could put the radio set used by SADL in the F-16, and link into the network to see where the ground units are located. The targeting pod and the SADL have made the squadron more suitable for the CAS mission."

ALERT MISSION

The 140th Wing maintains F-16s on alert 24/7, 365 days a year in support of North American Aerospace Defense Command's (NORAD) air sovereignty alert (ASA).

Buckley is one of 18 sites across the country that maintains aircraft on alert to deter, respond to, and if necessary, defeat airborne threats over the United States and Canada. The pilots that fly the alert mission are the last line of defence in a multi-layered system.

In its January 2012 report to Congressional Requesters the US Government Accountability Office gave the following details of the alert mission.

"Both Air Combat Command and the National Guard Bureau believe that Air National Guard units can conduct alert duty with less effect on overseas missions and at a lower cost than active-duty units. Consequently, Air National Guard units are on alert at 17 of the 18 ASA sites. In addition, units at all 18 ASA sites (ie, both Air National Guard and active-duty personnel) are dual-tasked to conduct both ASA operations and expeditionary missions.

"ASA operations consist of ground operations that take place before fighter aircraft take off, including such activities as maintaining the fighter aircraft. They also include those activities that may take place after a unit receives an alert from NORAD, but before the aircraft are airborne. For example, pilots and maintenance personnel may rush from their nearby lodging facility to the alert aircraft facility, where maintenance personnel conduct final preparations while the pilots sit in their aircraft awaiting further instruction (battle station). Alternatively, pilots may taxi the aircraft to the end of the runway and await further instruction (runway alert) or take off in response to the alert (scramble). Once aircraft take off, an Air National Guard pilot converts from Title 32 status under the command and control of the state governor to federal Title 10 status under the command and control of NORAD."

Lt Col Vanbeek said: "A lot of times we'll get suited up, which means putting on your G suit, harness and to be ready, but we don't go out to the jet at that point. We go to the command post to get more information on the situation. If, for example, it's a disruptive passenger, we don't have to launch.

"Sometimes we have to go to battle station, which means we go out to the jet, call in and get the information. Sometimes we actually start the jet up and taxi to the end of the runway and wait which is called runway alert. But as fiscal constraints get tighter, the number of scrambles gets less, but we do practise scrambles."

This commitment presents the wing's aircraft maintenance unit with the challenge of having maintainers on station all the time.

Lt Col Vanbeek explained that the bigger issue comes when the unit has to deploy. "There are different funding mechanisms that deem whether we take the whole squadron on deployment and have guys come in and sit alert at our home station while we are gone. You can't expect guys to always sit alert, when all their colleagues are deployed and making a difference to the country's need. That's one issue which the alert mission hamstrings us with in respect of an overseas operational mission."

THE BUCKET

Every 20 months, units such as the 140th Wing enter a vulnerability window to deploy, known as the bucket. Lt Col Vanbeek explained: "Whatever situations are going on in the world, while we're in the bucket we could be tasked

Loaded with CATM-120 AMRAAM and CATM-9X Sidewinder training missiles, a AAQ-33 Litening targeting pod and an ALQ-131 electronic countermeasures pod, F-16C 86-0345/CO lands at Nellis Air Force Base, Nevada after a Red Flag mission. Paul Ridgway

Colorado Air National Guard F-16Cs arrive at an air base in Jordan for Exercise Eager Lion. SMSgt John Rohrer/US Air National Guard

Mile High Militia

Paul Ridgway

to go. That means we have to be a 'jack of all trades' and must be trained in all of the roles we're capable of conducting. Nobody knows what's going to be needed so the AEF bucket drives our mission training."

The 120th FS last deployed to the US Central Command AOR on November 1, 2012 for a 60-day period when it replaced an F-15E Strike Eagle unit. This was unusual because the 120th FS deployed on its own for the full 60-day stretch and not part of an Air National Guard Rainbow Wing. The Rainbow concept involves more than one unit, each deploying for 30 days to cover the required timeframe. This is done to help traditional guardsmen get the required leave from their civilian jobs.

During continuation training the squadron has the ability to drop inert heavy weapons on the range at nearby Fort Carson, but must use the Utah Test and Training Range to employ live munitions during pre-deployment training. Consequently the squadron's pilots have plenty of experience in dropping live bombs during pre-deployment training and while flying combat missions when deployed.

Maintaining a set number of alert aircraft ready at all times and back-up aircraft available if any alert aircraft break presents a challenge for the 140th MXG. The challenge gets tougher when the wing is in the bucket, but support is also required to keep pilots qualified and be prepared to deploy a full complement of people and aircraft to an AOR.

REDEYE MAINTENANCE

Preparing an F-16 for the daily flight schedule takes about two-and-a-half hours every morning. The fighter squadron's flying schedule is issued at the start of each week and is based on the requirements of the 140th Operations Group (OG) and the ability of the 140th MXG to generate the number of aircraft required.

SMSgt John McCallick, a Maintenance Supervisor with the 140th MXG said that it's an ever-moving requirement to fly either air-to-air or air-to-ground missions. "Each task required by the operations group causes us work. If we're flying a slick phase without tanks [air-to-air] then we need to take tanks off the jets. If you change to an air-to-ground role we have to put tanks back on the jets. That's a couple of hours each side. Multiply that by the number of missions flown that day and it's a couple of days of work: that's on a good day. If aircraft come back broken, the specialists assigned to the maintenance squadron will troubleshoot, pinpoint and find out what the issue is, order the part and repair it."

However SMSgt McCallick said that ordering parts is something of a challenge. "We don't get new parts we get parts that have been overhauled at the depot and only 50% of those ordered work. We are against a timeline to train pilots versus a supply system that's old and takes time to deliver parts. Coupled with the complication of troubleshooting a 30-year-old aircraft, figuring out what the issue is, based on its upgraded configuration, makes the process a tried and trusted system."

The F-16 has undergone a couple of service life extension programmes. Today each aircraft is a modified hybrid but despite their current configuration they are similar and can all perform the same roles. Despite the similarity, the maintainers must conduct different upgrades at different times. This means the squadron might only have a certain number of aircraft at a time until the entire fleet is upgraded to the same standard, which is all dependent on funding.

Having different groups of aircraft in different configurations creates the need for a cherry picking exercise between the operations group and the maintenance squadron especially when pilots are training to deploy.

SMSgt McCallick explained: "If you have a two seat F-16, which is not desirable for a pilot because it can't achieve the turning performance required, even though you have x number of jets available, you actually have less than that number because of their individual configuration."

Spreading flight hours amongst specific airframes also presents a challenge. The problem is in part overcome by the air force 400-hour isochronal inspection process. This is tracked on a phase line: a graph that shows each aircraft and its flight hours and which ones are short and long on hours.

SMSgt McCallick said: "The production superintendent couples the details on the graph with which aircraft are broken, which ones need to be upgraded, and what the individual configuration and weapons requirements are, to try to avoid what's called a waterfall. The term is used when four jets roll into an isochronal phase at the same time. That's bad because each aircraft takes 30 days to complete, which impacts on operations."

Maintaining the fleet's average is a perpetual process. The same hectic planning continues every single day and must be co-ordinated to allow training and the alert

Mark Ayton

A Colorado Air National Guard F-16C at a deployed location within the US Central Command AOR loaded with two 1,000lb GBU-16 and two 500lb BLU-129/B laser-guided bombs. The BLU-129/B has a carbon fibre warhead casing designed to disintegrate and not fragment. A1C Nicholas Byers/US Air Force

mission to be supported. SMSgt McCallick, an experienced maintainer with 18 years experience, said the maintenance crews never really feel a sense of relief or that they have achieved the goal.

MAINTAINING COMPONENTS

There should be no surprise that as the F-16 and its components get older, the aircraft gets harder to maintain: even more so under the current budget constraints. These are the two dynamics that affect maintenance on all of the aircraft's major components: avionics, electrical-environmental, egress, engine (propulsion), fuel systems, hydraulics, radar, targeting and ECM pods, and software. Each one is maintained by a specialised shop.

To appreciate the necessity of maintenance work in general it's important to consider the attention paid to certain metrics by the commanders of each air force major command. How many aircraft are in the fleet? How many are serviceable? How many engines are available? What's the mission? What's the minimum number of aircraft required?

Based on the considerations listed, it's imperative for all maintainers to report accurate information about each aircraft and its maintenance status. They do this by tagging the work unit code and the specific item. "This must be done correctly because the bottom feeds the top," said SMSgt McCallick.

The US Air Force made a major change to the aircraft inspection system listed in Air Force Instruction 90-201. Today's criteria require the maintenance group to remain at a steady state of preparedness so that anyone in the chain of command knows the exact status of each jet.

Buckley's engine shop falls under a CERF (Centralised Engine Repair Facility) with a specific number of engines allocated for a certain number of units. The 140th Maintenance Squadron has a primary authorised inventory (a specific number) of engines and spares. If at any time it requires more, the CERF has to supply the additional engines. If a TCTO (Time Compliance Technical Order) is issued notifying an engine fault, that will drive a TCI (Time Change Item) detailing what modifications are required on each engine. The local engine shop may be able to complete some of the work, but some may have to be undertaken by another facility. Therefore a TCI will drive how the shop monitors each engine, which determines the availability of each unit.

The avionics shop is the most heavily tasked within the 140th MXG. Ninety percent of all maintenance write-ups are with avionics hardware, such as a broken wire, a line replaceable unit or a bus board. In addition, the avionics shop is also responsible for maintaining the Block 30 F-16 APG-68 radar.

BUCKLEY OPS

On a day-to-day basis, the 120th FS uses air space located to the east of Buckley. The areas used were first allocated as military operating areas (MOAs) when the parent 140th Wing flew the F-100 Super Sabre in the 1960s. Today the squadron's Block 30 F-16s have a long-range air-to-air capability (the AIM-120 AMRAAM missile) which presents a need for bigger areas in which to practise tactical intercepts. The challenge for the wing is to try to expand the airspace which is made more difficult when the area impacts on commercial air traffic bound for Denver Stapleton International Airport. The process of expanding the size of the existing MOAs is under way.

At the other end of the training requirements is low-level flying. This is still practised when the squadron is in the bucket, but the frequency of this kind of training is not as regular as it used to be because of emerging surface-to-air threats. Lt Col Vanbeek explained: "Usually we know we're going against specific ground threats, so we've got to remain out of its engagement zone. If there's no such threat we might fly at low level."

FALCON AIR MEET

In July 2013 the 140th Wing deployed to Jordan to attend Exercise Eager Lion and the Falcon Air Meet. This is Jordan's biggest exercise and has two components: an alert scramble, including air-to-air interdiction, and a bombing competition. Both components are graded: aircrew for the alert scramble and maintenance and ammo crews for building and loading munitions in the bombing competition.

Deploying a guard unit to the event, enables the US Air Force to provide a unit with plenty of experience. The average number of flight hours flown in the F-16 by

Mile High Militia

all 120th Fighter Squadron pilots is 1,500 hours. All of the squadron's pilot cadre have dropped bombs in combat during deployments to the US Central Command AOR. This means that the US Air Force is able to help the Royal Jordanian Air Force with its training goals by providing instructor pilots to fly upgrade sorties with the Jordanian pilots.

RED FLAG 2014

The 120th FS deployed to Red Flag in February 2014 in accordance with the air force requirement to do so within a certain window leading up to the bucket.

According to Brigadier General Stephen Whiting, Vice Commander of the United States Air Force Warfare Center: "Red Flag is the premiere training venue where the air force integrates air, space, and cyber effects in a joint and coalition environment at the tactical and operational levels of war."

Brig Gen Whiting also said use of the unique assets of Nellis, which include the 2.9-million acre Nevada Test and Training Range and the Combined Air and Space Operations Center-Nellis, along with the Space Test and Training Range and the virtual and constructive environments are used to extend the simulated battlespace over an even larger area. Red Flag continues to improve on its objective of providing the first ten combat missions for operational crews, maintenance, and support team members.

During the flag Lt Col Vanbeek was mission commander on a large strike package comprising 85 aircraft. "It's the closest thing to the stress of combat because you're working 12-hour days and it's as real as it can get other than combat. Many of the missions include live weapons which have to be de-conflicted with other aircraft and people on the range. It's one of the few places where you can actually see a missile being shot at you and lock you up. Based on the nature of the training, the air space available, the threat lay-down and the number of assets participating, there's no other place that can offer that kind of training," he said.

Maintainers assigned to the 140th MXG had to counter cyber threats on the Nellis flight line during Red Flag 14-1. The objective was to test their ability to support flight operations in what the air force calls a CDO (contested, degraded or operationally limited) environment. The Red Flag planners wanted to ensure the maintenance teams deployed for the exercise are able to problem-solve and respond if they are faced with a compromise in technology or cyber threat. The scenarios were devised to train the maintainers in a similar way to pilots and included academics on cyber vulnerabilities, information operations and CDO-related threats.

Lt Col Neff said the 120th FS was tasked with air interdiction and close air support roles during Red Flag 14-1. "We were only able to drop 24 Mk82 slick [dumb] bombs due to weather and airspace restrictions but in general we performed very well on the air-to-ground missions."

TOTAL FORCE INTEGRATION

As part of the US Air Force Total Force Initiative, four active-duty pilots, an experienced flight commander and four lieutenants, arrived at the 140th Wing in the last quarter of 2014. They are now assigned to the 120th Fighter Squadron and reside at Buckley. The initiative creates a means for the active-duty lieutenants to learn from experienced Guardsmen and pass that knowledge on to their squadron colleagues when they return to an active-duty squadron. According to Lt Col Vanbeek, many active-duty pilots that have undertaken a TFI tour with the guard want to return later in their careers.
Mark Ayton

Two 120th Fighter Squadron Block 30 F-16Cs perform a pairs-departure from Buckley Air Force Base. Each aircraft is loaded with BDU-33 practice bombs. Mark Ayton

F-16 Falcon Still in the Fight

All images Simon Bullimore unless noted

The 169th Fighter Wing, based at McEntire Air National Guard Base, South Carolina, is equipped with two dozen Block 52 F-16s. It is the only combat-coded wing in the US Air Force to fly the Block 52.

Known as the Swamp Foxes, the 169th Fighter Wing (FW) is the longest serving F-16 unit in the Air National Guard. It transitioned to the Block 52 in 1994 after flying the Block 10 F-16A since 1983.

HARDWARE

Its primary mission set is Suppression of Enemy Air Defences (SEAD) and the Destruction of Enemy Air Defences (DEAD) subset. Among the many munitions employed by the Block 52 is the AGM-88 High-speed Anti-Radiation Missile (HARM) and its associated ASQ-213A targeting system (HTS) for the SEAD role. Both the missile and the HTS integrate with the aircraft's M6.2 Operational Flight Program software.

Explaining the hardware the 169th FW's Vice Commander, Colonel Nicholas Gentile, said the crew station does not have a large, high-definition screen for viewing targeting images, something that is expected to be fitted from 2017. "The extra screen will enable pilots to view more of the aircraft's sensor feeds simultaneously. We currently train to prioritise them. When you are making an air-to-air sweep you want to see your radar and tactical situation display in conjunction with those generated by the targeting pod and HARM system. We don't yet have sensor fusion, like an F-35 or an F-22 but the situational display gives a very basic fusion of information and that's extremely useful," he said.

The 169th FW is also working with Air Combat Command (ACC) on integrating an active electronically scanned array (AESA) radar system on to some F-16s. "We're reviewing the technology out there right now for application into Block 30s, 40s and 50s and 52s. The aircraft that are going to fly for another 25 years will need that capability in an electronic countermeasure environment to survive. We would like to be able to do that and use an AESA radar for all its other capabilities, whether that's SAR [synthetic aperture radar] mapping, jamming or any of the things that an AESA radar can do simultaneously that we don't currently have in the Block 52."

Sourcing an AESA radar system for the F-16 fleet is an active US Air Force initiative but it is not CAPES, the Combat Avionics Programmed Extension Suite, or a revival of it. One element from CAPES, a service life extension programme, is going ahead and will facilitate an AESA radar system.

"ACC has approved the initial look. We're getting a couple of AESA radar units

> Written in 2015, some of the technical aspects discussed within this chapter have been superseded or now come to fruition.

Swamp

F-16 Falcon Still in the Fight

> "When you join the unit, you're not just coming to do a job you're coming to be part of the culture"
>
> MSgt John Pearsall, Training Manager with the 169th Maintenance Group

A pilot prepares the cockpit before getting in.

under way in the region," said the vice commander.

The wing's deployment schedule continued. In November 2014 it went to Naval Air Station Fallon, Nevada, to work with Carrier Air Wing 7 providing the SEAD element during its Strike Fighter Advanced Readiness Program training.

The air force is the only US service still conducting the reactive SEAD mission, the US Navy's EA-18G Growler force specialises in the electronic attack and jamming mission set. But the two services work hand-in-hand. "We mission plan them [EA-18G Growlers] in and we count on them being at certain places and doing certain things to accomplish the mission. Working together is a real force multiplier," said Col Gentile.

In March the wing sent ten aircraft to Davis-Monthan Air Force Base for Exercise Long Rifle. Flying from McEntire, the aircraft flew across the United States with air-refuelling support and conducted a strike in the Barry Goldwater range in western Arizona. Opposing fighters protecting the target meant the South Carolina Guardsmen had to fight their way in, drop live bombs and fight their way out before recovering to Davis-Monthan for the debrief.

The amount of training undertaken by the wing and its mission preparedness is evident from the level of experience of the maintainers and pilots serving with the 169th FW. With more than 30 years' experience of F-16 operations gained from numerous peacetime and combat deployments around the world, it should be no surprise that the wing is regularly called upon to answer its nation's call. The Swamp Foxes brilliantly epitomise the Air National Guard. *Mark Ayton*

F-16 Falcon Still in the Fight

Atacama Falcons

For years, Chile had a relatively small air force, given its size and the border problems with neighbours Argentina, Bolivia and Peru. But the economic growth of the country since the 1980s and a protagonist approach to regional politics led to a new way of thinking that's seen increased defence spending – making Chilean armed forces comparable to its neighbours' and making them a modern and efficient military power.

At the beginning of the 1990s, the Fuerza Aérea de Chile (FACh, Chilean Air Force) started planning for the replacement of its combat aircraft by launching Proyecto Caza 2000 (Project Fighter 2000). The objective was to replace its Hawker Hunters, Mirage 50s and F-5E Tiger IIs with a single type.

To fulfil the requirement a fighter competition began, for which the FACh pre-selected the Lockheed Martin F-16 Fighting Falcon, the Saab JAS 39 Gripen, the Dassault Mirage 2000 and the Sukhoi Su-30 *Flanker* – announcing it would buy about 100 aircraft.

Evaluation of the four began in 1994 in what was considered to be the most ambitious fighter competition in Latin America for years. Manufacturers were ambitious in thinking the winner could potentially also gain contracts from Argentina and Brazil, which were both looking to replace their combat aircraft. Brazil selected the JAS 39E Gripen in December 2013 and Argentina has still to launch a competition.

BUDGET CUTS

Chile's ambitious programme soon faced an age old problem – lack of funds. That was nothing new: it's an issue that constantly affects Latin American procurement.

Delays to the project started. The idea of replacing all types in FACh service with a single type was placed on ice and priority given to the fighters that needed urgent replacement.

The Chilean Government bought 25 former Belgian Air Force Mirage Vs to replace the Hunters of Grupo 8 at Base Aérea Cerro Moreno at Antofagasta, in the Atacama desert in the north of the country. The Mirages were named Elkans in FACh service.

Meanwhile the FACh pursued its quest for a new model –the former Belgian Mirages were only a stopgap solution because the Elkans and the existing Mirage 50s due to retire from active service before 2010.

By the end of the 1990s the FACh was interested in Lockheed Martin F-16 Fighting Falcons, new or used, especially when the US Government approved the sale of the model to Chile in August of 1997. Budgets were still tight, which meant the FACh fighter procurement office had to choose between a small number of new, or a larger number of second-hand, aircraft.

SELECTION

After successive pauses in the competition, on December 27, 2000 Chilean president Ricardo Lagos announced the winner of the Caza 2000 competition was Lockheed Martin's Block 50/52 F-16. The plan was to buy either 12 or 16 aircraft for up to $600 million. The US Government then announced it would not sell AIM-120 AMRAAM missiles to Chile, an important part of the FACh's request.

The FACh and Lockheed Martin signed a letter of intent on February 1, 2002 for ten Block 50 F-16s (six single-seat F-16Cs and four two-seat F-16Ds) for $547 million – including General Electric F110-GE-129 engines. The aircraft can use AGM-84 Harpoon anti-ship and AGM-88 HARM (High-speed Anti-Radiation Missiles) and Joint Direct Attack Munitions. They are equipped with Northrop Grumman APG-68(V)5 radars and VHSIC (very high-speed integrated circuit technology).

Lockheed Martin announced it had signed a $320 million contract with the US Air Force on May 22, 2003 for the sale of the ten Block 50 F-16 aircraft to Chile under the Peace Puma Foreign Military Sale programme. Construction of the first aircraft, F-16C 851, began at Lockheed Martin's Fort Worth plant in October 2004. It was rolled-out on April 13, 2005, took its maiden flight on June 23 and then remained in the US to certify its systems in accordance with the FACh's requirements.

The first two aircraft to be delivered, F-16Ds 858 and 859, arrived at Santiago de Chile on January 31, 2006 and were assigned to the re-established Grupo 3 de Aviación at Base Aérea Los Cóndores near Iquique in northern Chile. The first four FACh pilots were trained at Luke Air Force Base, Arizona. The FACh F-16 made its public debut in FIDAE 2006 at Santiago de Chile International Airport in late March.

To increase the new aircraft's strike roles, on August 6, 2006 the FACh announced it was buying ten AGM-84 Harpoon II anti-ship missiles for $15 million, to give the air force a maritime strike capability.

The last two single-seat F-16Cs arrived at Base Aérea Los Cóndores on March 14 2007 to complete Grupo 3's fleet.

After 12 months' intensive training, the FACh force – comprising Grupo 3 and Grupo 8 (by then equipped with former Dutch F-16AMs, see Elkan Replacement) – demonstrated its operational capabilities during Exercise Newen, a joint training event flown with units assigned to the Air Combat Command's 12th Air Force in April 2008. US Air Force aircraft involved were an HC-130, a KC-10A, a KC-135R, three 457th Fighter Squadron F-16Cs from Naval Air Station Joint Reserve Base Fort Worth and three 391st Fighter Squadron F-15Es from Mountain Home Air Force Base, Idaho.

During the exercise the FACh F-16 pilots trained with US Air Force tankers, the first time they had undertaken air refuelling with boom-equipped aircraft: the FACh's Boeing 707 tanker was only fitted with hose-and-drogue.

F-16 Falcon Still in the Fight

Two Chilean Block 50 F-16Cs over the Atacama Desert in the northern part of the country during a mission from Iquique.

> The first Chilean Block 50 F-16C was rolled-out from Lockheed Martin's Fort Worth plant on April 13, 2005

ELKAN REPLACEMENT

Meanwhile, the FACh continued looking for a replacement for its remaining Elkans and began negotiations in November 2004 with the Koninklijke Luchtmacht (Royal Netherlands Air Force) for 18 second-hand Block 15 F-16MLUs (11 single-seat F-16AMs and seven two-seat F-16BMs).

All were built by Fokker in the 1980s and had undergone a mid-life update (MLU) between 1997 and 2003 at Woensdrecht Air Base, bringing them up to a configuration equivalent to a US Air Force Block 50 F-16.

The modifications included a new signal processor for the Northrop Grumman APG-66 radar, a BAE Systems APX-113(V)2 Advanced Identification Friend or Foe Combined Interrogator/Transponder, multi-function displays and the facility to use helmet-mounted cueing systems.

An F-16AM equipped with a Rafael Litening navigation and target pod.

The F-16MLU could also employ AIM-120 AMRAAM missiles, the CBU-87 Combined Effects Munition and Paveway series laser-guided bombs. The MLU also included Falcon Up, a structural upgrade designed to extend the airframe's service life to 8,000 hours.

The contract for 18 aircraft, valued at $185m and signed on December 16, 2005, included $7.5m for Lockheed Martin to remove the M2 Operational Flight Program (OFP) software. The aircraft kept the automatic target hand-off and target designation systems – and received improvements to its digital terrain system.

Eight aircraft (five F-16AMs and three F-16BMs, including two air spares) took off from Twenthe Air Base on September 4, 2006 with KDC-10 tanker T-235 on the first leg of their delivery to Antofagasta, where they arrived on September 7 having stopped at Gando (Canary Islands) and

The Chilean Government's decision to base all of its F-16s at Antofagasta and Iquique in the north of the country is to counter any threats posed by its northern neighbour Peru.

Recife (Brazil). They were presented to Chile's then president, Michelle Bachelet, the following day.

Each jet had its rudder painted blue with a white star and a Dutch roundel in low-visibility colours. A supporting Il-76 was chartered to carry spares, a Dutch pilot and 11 technicians who flew to Chile to help introduce the F-16 to FACh service. All eight aircraft were assigned to Grupo 8 with the Elkans.

The US authorised the sale of 28 LAU-129/A guided missile launchers for AIM-9 Sidewinder and AIM-120 AMRAAM missiles. The AMRAAM sale was authorised but the weapons were not delivered immediately, leaving Chile with the option to buy Israeli-built Rafael Derby and short-range Python 4 air-to-air missiles (now in Chilean service on the F-5E). Two further batches of F-16s arrived in country on April 16 and June 7, 2007.

The remaining Mirage V Elkans had been retired on December 27, 2006, leaving the F-16 as the only fighter in service with Grupo 8.

MORE AIRCRAFT

The Dutch Government made a new offer in 2007 for 16 more F-16s (in a $160 million deal) as replacements for the Mirage 50 Panteras, and at the end of 2009 agreement was reached for the delivery of 18 MLU-standard F-16AMs.

F-16AMs and an F-16BM equipped with air combat manoeuvring instrumentation pods taxiing at Natal Air Base, Brazil.

F-16 Falcon Still in the Fight

> **In late October 2012, the FACh deployed its F-16s outside Chile for the first time to Natal Air Base in northern Brazil**

By then, a plan to retire the F-5 fleet was on hold, and the F-16s were sent to Punta Arenas, where the Panteras were operating. Once deployed to Chile's most southern air base, the F-16s encountered problems caused by stones blown onto the runway and taxiways because of strong winds. This made the operation of the F-16, with its low air-intake, very dangerous and the decision was taken to re-assign the F-16s elsewhere.

Consequently this second tranche of former Dutch F-16s was assigned to Grupo 7 at Antofagasta. The 18 jets, delivered in three groups of six, arrived in Chile on November 4, 2010, April 8, 2011 and September 1.

They were all configured with a modular mission computer loaded with the M4 OFP bombs. The FACh uses the AAQ-28 Litening pod to laser-designate targets.

Unguided munitions used are the Mk82 and the French SAMP BL70 general-purpose bombs.

UPGRADES

Chile's Ministerio de Defensa contracted US company ITT Exelis to upgrade the ALQ-211(V)4 AIDEWS (Advanced Integrated Defensive Electronic Warfare Suite), which provides the pilot with what Exelis calls advanced situational awareness fed by a suite of sub-systems that include a digital radar warning receiver, high and low-band jamming and countermeasures dispensers.

F-16AM FACh 738, the first aircraft to be completed at Santiago, was delivered on June 11, 2012. The upgrade is currently delayed because the structural condition of the airframes was worse than expected, leading senior FACh officers to lodge complaints with the Dutch.

At 13:00pm local time on March 30, 2012, F-16AM FACh 735 made an emergency landing at Cerro Moreno when the landing gear retracted, damaging the aircraft's belly. This was the third such accident involving a FACh F-16, but no information about the other two has been released by the Chilean Air Force.

NOTABLE OPS

In March 2010 unidentified aircraft were detected in Chilean airspace close to the

Chile's Block 50 F-16s are the most capable variants of the type in Latin America.

software – enabling them to carry two types of anti-radiation missile, the AGM-45 Shrike and the AGM-88 HARM, and the AIM-9 Sidewinder air-to-air missile.

Other improvements were Link 16 data link and the ability to use the AAQ-33 Sniper advanced targeting pod. Some Chilean Air Force sources suggest the aircraft supplied in the first tranche were upgraded to the same configuration once they had arrived in Chile.

The FACh's fleet of MLU and Block 50 F-16s is armed with an arsenal of French, Israeli and US weapons. Air-to-air missiles are the short-range AIM-9P/AIM-9L Sidewinder and Rafael Python 4; beyond-visual-range types are the AIM-120B, AIM-120C2 and AIM-120C5 AMRAAM and the Rafael Derby, which is only used by the MLU aircraft.

Air-to-surface missiles are the AGM-65 Maverick and the anti-ship AGM-84 Harpoon. Laser-guided bombs differ depending on the variant: Block 50 aircraft use 500lb (227kg) GBU-12 Paveway IIs and the MLU jets use the Israeli Lizard M2 and M4 guidance kits on 500lb and 1,000lb (454kg) general-purpose bombs.

Because each tranche of aircraft supplied to the FACh had a different configuration, and those in the first tranche had not received the Pacer Amstel modification to extend service lifetime (further than the MLU structural enhancement), the air force launched Project FITS in a bid to bring parity to the whole fleet. Modification work in Chile was supported by Dutch company Daedalus, which trained FACh personnel and worked with them on the aircraft at Cerro Moreno Air Base.

Work involved installation of the Falcon Star modifications (structural changes that were the basis of the Pacer Amstel programme) and some components from Falcon Up not installed in the Netherlands during the MLU.

The first aircraft, F-16AM FACh 728, upgraded by Dutch personnel with the Chileans learning during the process, made its first flight on January 6, 2011.

Two more aircraft were delivered in June and those arriving later were modified by Chilean personnel, with Dutch supervision, at Enaer's facility at Santiago's International Airport.

country's northern coast, coming from the sea. A Casa A-36 on a training flight was sent to investigate while two Grupo 7 F-16s were scrambled.

Shortly before intercepting, the pilots were informed the intruders were F/A-18E Super Hornets from the USS Carl Vinson, under way in international waters. The US Navy jets were ordered to leave Chilean airspace because they had not been authorised to fly there. The A-36 was ordered to return to its base and the two F-16s continued patrolling the limit of Chilean waters while the US jets left the area.

That year, Grupo 10 at Santiago de Chile received the first of three KC-135E Stratotankers purchased from the US and started regular air-refuelling missions with the F-16s.

In late October, the FACh deployed its F-16s outside Chile for the first time to take part in Cruzex V, a Brazilian exercise staged from two bases in the northeast of the country. The international event also involved the air forces of Argentina, Brazil, France, Uruguay and the United States.

F-16 Falcon Still in the Fight

Five F-16Cs and two F-16Ds flew from their bases in Iquique (Grupo 3) and three F-16AMs from Antofagasta (Grupo 8) flew with a KC-135E tanker to Natal Air Base in Brazil, where they operated with French Air Force Dassault Rafales and Mirage 2000s, US Air Force F-16Cs, Uruguayan A-37Bs and all the tactical types flown by the Brazilian Air Force.

Two years later, an F-16C and two F-16Ds, supported by a KC-135E, from Iquique flew to Kelly Field in San Antonio, Texas, to train with the F-16-equipped 182nd Fighter Squadron 'Lone Star Gunfighters' – the flying squadron of Texas Air National Guard's 149th Fighter Wing. The Chileans flew more than 4,000nm (7,500km) on the longest non-stop flight performed by Latin American combat aircraft to date.

Two Grupo 7 F-16AMs deployed to Santiago de Chile on January 21, 2013 to protect the airspace over the city during the first meeting of the leaders of Latin American, the Caribbean and the European Union. It was the first time FACh F-16s had deployed loaded with live AIM-120 AMRAAM missiles and a Litening pod.

F-16s assigned to Grupo 8 deployed to Natal Air Base, Brazil that November for Exercise Cruzex, during which they flew with US Air Force and Venezuelan F-16s – the first occasion when American and Venezuelan F-16s had participated in the same exercise, although both elements performed different missions: the US in air-to-ground roles and the Venezuelans on combat air patrols and escort. The FACh's F-16s flew in all roles.

The most recent exercise involving FACh F-16s was Salitre III at Antofagasta and Iquique in October 2014. Aircraft from Grupo 7 flew as Blue Air with F-5Es of Grupo 12, six Argentine Air Force A-4AR Fightinghawks, four Brazilian Air Force F-5EMs, three Uruguayan Air Force Cessna A-37B Dragonflies and six F-16Cs of the Texas Air National Guard's 149th Fighter Wing. Red Air was provided by FACh F-16s from Grupo 3 and Grupo 8 based at Iquique.

To test its long range strike capability, the FACh sent eight Fighting Falcons (four F-16Cs and four F-16Ds) from Iquique to Santiago on September 19, 2014 for Chilean independence day. They rendezvoused with a KC-135E, refuelled over the Andes mountains despite turbulence, made a flypast over the city, rendezvoused with the tanker a second time and recovered back to Iquique at the end of a 1,600nm (3,000km) round trip.

Today the F-16 is the FACh's main combat aircraft, with superior performance to fighters operated by neighbouring nations. Argentina continues to use Mirage IIIs and Mirage Vs, IAI Fingers and A-4AR Fightinghawks while Peru flies variants of first-generation MiG-29 Fulcrums and Mirage 2000Ps.

Chilean F-16 squadrons train in roles including air defence, escort, air-to-ground strike and anti-ship. They are responsible for protecting all Chilean airspace from the northern border with Bolivia and Peru down to Puerto Montt; F-5 squadrons cover the southern part of the country.

Until the Chilean Navy's air arm received its C235PM Persuaders (also armed with Harpoons), the nation's only maritime strike

Chile's first Block 50 F-16C FACh 851, refuelling from a KC-135E Stratotanker over the Andes.

> **Chilean F-16 squadrons train in roles including air defence, escort, air-to-ground strike and anti-ship**

capability was provided by naval Super Puma helicopters armed with Exocet missiles. The AGM-84 Harpoon is the first anti-ship missile to be used by the FACh and the F-16, being faster and more agile, is a more appropriate launch platform for the anti-ship strike role.

Tensions between Chile and Argentina are currently low, but the country still has some disputes with Bolivia and Peru.

Bolivia still claims part of the territories lost in a war with Chile in the late nineteenth century, but its air force presents little threat, its fighter force comprising Lockheed T-33s and Hongdu K-8 trainers.

Peru and Chile had a territorial dispute over the sovereignty of an area of the Pacific Ocean, the International Court of Justice at The Hague accepting a case brought by Peru in January 2008. Under a final ruling on January 27, 2014, Chile lost control of part of the area it had previously claimed, which was then ceded to Peru.

Despite the easing of tensions the two nations still have a complicated relationship. Should ill feeling increase, the Peruvian Air Force presents a potential threat with its Mirage 2000s and modernised MiG-29SMPs – and its plans to buy new aircraft. **Santiago Rivas**

Greece was the first F-16 operator to combine the 'big spine' dorsal modification found on the Block 52+ F-16D with Conformal Fuel Tanks. *Tom Gibbons*

F-16 Falcon Still in the Fight

Zeus

Greece has played a pivotal role defending NATO's southern flank since joining the alliance in 1952. In addition, the Hellenic Air Force is regularly called upon to defend territorial rights in the Aegean against Turkey, a fellow NATO member.

The investment made by Greece in the F-16, that culminated in the procurement of what at the time (2010) was the latest Advanced Block 52+ variant, has been necessary to secure and defend territorial rights in concert with other air force, navy and army aviation assets. One senior pilot F-16 pilot told the author: "We are on constant alert throughout Greece. We have to be because of the number of daily incursions in our air space by the Turkish Air Force. We've had 40 incursions in one day with the total number of engagements running into thousands."

The relationship between Greece and Turkey has improved, with mutual respect between pilots. There is, however, no compromise over border control. Air policing is the bread and butter role for the Hellenic Air Force's (HAF) Block 50 and Block 52 F-16s every day of the year.

F-16 procurement was the most ambitious fighter programme ever undertaken by Greece. All aircraft were supplied under four US Foreign Military Sales programmes called Peace Xenia. The first Block 30 F-16C entered HAF service in 1989.

F-16 Falcon Still in the Fight

PEACE XENIA PROGRAMMES

Peace Xenia I	40 Block 30 F-16C and F-16D	1989 to 1990
Peace Xenia II	40 Block 50 F-16C and F-16D	1997 to 1998
Peace Xenia III	60 Block 52+ F-16C and F-16D	2002 to 2004
Peace Xenia IV	30 Block 52+ Advanced F-16C and F-16D	2009 to 2010

ROLES

All HAF F-16 squadrons conduct air defence (ADF) and air-to-ground bomber (A2G) roles while 335 Squadron specialises in reconnaissance (RECCE) and 343 Squadron in Suppression of Enemy Air Defences (SEAD), each using specific systems and weapons. Specialised roles are allocated to specific squadrons simply because the HAF cannot afford to maintain each squadron in all roles, but strives to exploit every aspect of the F-16's capabilities.

A 343 Squadron pilot gave a good example: "There is no such thing as a standard SEAD mission. It really does depend on the target and factors such as intelligence. SEAD assets are always high value. Once our missiles are launched, we switch to ADF to protect our other strike aircraft. It's a complex mission. One we demonstrated during our first Red Flag in November 2008 which impressed American personnel."

Pilot training missions have multi-role tasking to meet all combat objectives, switching between ADF and A2G and for the specialised squadrons changing to SEAD and RECCE during the same mission. To maintain preparedness, all HAF squadrons fly a daily joint training exercise involving other assets that include different aircraft types, surface-to air-missiles (SAMs), command reporting centres (CRCs), and often with other force elements from the navy and army.

SQUADRON ALLOCATION AND ROLES

Block 30 F-16C/F-16D	111 Combat Wing	330 Squadron	Nea Anchialos Air Base
Block 50 F-16C/F-16D	111 Combat Wing	341 and 347 Squadron	Nea Anchialos Air Base
Block 52 F-16C/F-16D	110 Combat Wing	337 Squadron	Larisa Air Base
Block 52+ F-16C/F-16D	115 Combat Wing	340 and 343 Sqn	Souda Air Base
Block 52+ Adv F-16C/D	116 Combat Wing	335 Squadron	Araxos Air Base

BLOCK 52+

The US Block system defines the configuration of each variant of the F-16. Differences between each Block include the avionics, the engine variant and conformal fuel tanks (CFTs).

The consensus among HAF pilots interviewed by the author is you have to be an excellent pilot to take full advantage of the Block 52+ aircraft. Experience to be able to cope with all the inputs required during the execution of a mission is essential.

HAF Block 52 aircraft are visually distinguishable from earlier variants by their special 'metallic' paintwork developed under the US Have Glass programme. The paint absorbs and scatters some radiation to reduce the aircraft's radar signature. One pilot confirmed the impact on aircraft signature, noting the distorted radar interference when tracking his own aircraft compared to the clarity found when tracking a Block 30 or Block 50. The paint feels rough to touch, like sand paper. Maintenance crew assert it is extremely difficult to clean.

The HAF was the first customer to combine the dorsal spine and CFTs. The dorsal spine is only installed on the two-seat F-16D while CFTs can be used by both the single-seat F-16C and the F-16D.

The dorsal spine houses an avionics compartment containing all the systems fitted to a single-seat F-16C plus additional equipment, including chaff and flare dispensers.

The aft cockpit can display mission-critical information, as one 335 Squadron pilot explained: "During complex missions this greatly enhances the pilot's situational awareness, flight safety and the formation's combat effectiveness. The aft cockpit is missionised in a similar way to our F-4s from where the second pilot acts as a weapons system operator controlling multi-function displays, sensors and weapons independently of the pilot."

Conformal fuel tanks hold an additional 3,000lb of fuel (450 gallons), provide greater range, longer loiter time, and can be used in place of external wing tanks.

From a combat perspective there are very few aerodynamic concerns with CFTs. An experienced Block 52+ Instructor Pilot from 340 Squadron told the author: "CFTs produce no drag on the aircraft and there are no big differences in its handling characteristics at all. Handling in the air is excellent. Like many pilots, my choice would be to fly with CFTs because the aircraft is extremely stable even when they are full of fuel. The extra weight of the fuel requires an additional 400 to 500 feet of runway and 10 to 12 miles per hour extra speed to get airborne. Range and duration are increased substantially, which is critical for us especially during air-to-ground missions."

In 2010, 335 Squadron based at Araxos Air Base in Southern Greece received the last of its 30 Block 52+ Advanced aircraft. All images Ian Harding unless noted

Two Block 52+ Advanced F-16Cs assigned to 335 Squadron based at Araxos Air Base in Southern Greece. The aircraft nearest to the camera is fitted with Conformal Fuel Tanks.

F-16 Falcon Still in the Fight

En route Red Flag 2008, 343 Squadron Block 52+ F-16s took-off from Keflavik, Iceland, for Goose Bay, Canada with 18,000lb of fuel for a 3½ hour, 1,350 nautical mile unrefuelled flight across the North Atlantic. 343 Squadron/Hellenic Air Force

Based at Araxos, 335 Squadron's Block 52+ Advanced F-16s specialise in the RECCE role using the UTC Aerospace Systems' DB-110 reconnaissance sensor.

Another instructor pilot assigned to 343 Squadron described the Block 52+ as very stable at low level with CFTs. "They do impact slightly on the turning capability of the jet but the aircraft accelerates quicker with them fitted because there is no drag; we call this 'drag zero'. That said, CFTs can create some handling difficulties when air refuelling," he said.

Each version of the Block 52+ (standard and advanced) has a bigger fuel and weapon payload capacity. The aircraft are fitted with nine stations (six for weapons and three for external fuel tanks), improved avionics and sensors, colour cockpit displays and pilot interfaces, and a modern internal electronic countermeasures system. Both versions are equipped with the Advanced Self-Protection Integrated Suite comprising the Northrop Grumman ALR-93 radar warning receiver and electronic warfare controller, the Raytheon ALQ-187 RF jammer, and the BAE Systems ALE-47 airborne countermeasures dispenser system for chaff and flares.

Both versions of the Block 52+ can carry two 600 gallon (4,000lb) external fuel tanks, one each on stations four and eight, which add 30% more range compared with the earlier 370 gallon (2,400lb) tanks, and a standard 300 gallon (2,000lb) centre line tank.

The three-tank configuration served 343 Squadron well during their outward leg to Nellis Air Force Base, Nevada for Exercise Red Flag in 2008. During one of six legs, their aircraft departed Keflavik, Iceland, with 18,000lb (2,700 gallons) of fuel for an incredible 3½ hour, 1,350 nautical mile (2,500km) un-refuelled journey to Goose Bay, Canada.

This particular route is rarely, if ever, attempted unsupported by tankers. The six crew members from 343 Squadron deserve high praise for completing the flight. The return leg was supported by tankers.

All HAF Block 52+ F-16s use the Northrop Grumman APG-68(V)9 multimode radar. "There is just no comparison with the APG-68(V)5 used by the Block 50," one pilot explained.

With increased speeds of processing data and memory capacity over the APG-68(V)7

The two resident units, 341 and 347 Squadrons, based at Nea Anchialos Air Base hold QRA to cover northern Greece.

F-16 Falcon Still in the Fight

and (V)8, the (V)9 has enhanced detection range of up to 30% and the ability to track single and multiple targets in both air-to-air and air-to-ground modes.

A synthetic aperture radar mode allows the pilot to locate and recognise ground targets from considerable distances and is able to generate weapon-quality coordinates for GPS-guided GBU-31 Joint Direct Attack Munitions. This provides the HAF with an all-weather, precision-strike capability from a stand-off range.

The effectiveness of the radar was confirmed by a senior pilot. "The radar enables us to accurately deliver precision-guided weapons autonomously in all weathers to different targets. Its target detection range is very impressive and improves our beyond visual range capability. Multi-function displays and night vision capability in the cockpit also give our pilots a lot of information on multiple targets in a battle scenario which we regularly practice. JHMCS [Joint Helmet-Mounted Cueing System] enables them to aim sensors and weapons wherever they are looking when 'heads-up' without having to look down into the cockpit during air-to-air combat which is always tense," he said.

Block 52+ aircraft have an NVG (night vision goggles) capability, and when paired with the JHMCS enhances the capability of the pilot and aircraft even further.

Communication systems fitted in the Block 52+ are multi-channel VHF, UHF and HF radios (which must be used separately), satellite communication and Link 16 data link. The latter provides secure, jam-resistant, high-volume data exchange on a multi-node network. The Advanced Block 52+ is also equipped with two radios that are interchangeable.

Pilots have a passive data modem which allows up to four aircraft to exchange data about air threats without the need for voice communication, improving situational awareness for the pilot while helping to build confidence during air-to-air combat.

Autonomous identification of airborne targets is provided by the combined interrogator/transponder, which maximises the launch range of radar-guided air-to-air missiles at distances beyond visual range.

MISSILES AND MUNITIONS

The multi-role Block 52+ F-16C has an impressive arsenal of air-to-air and air-to-ground missiles, precision-guided munitions, targeting and reconnaissance systems.
- *Air-to-air missiles: AIM-9 Sidewinder, AIM-120 AMRAAM, and the AIM-2000 IRIS-T (Infra Red Imaging System-Tail with thrust vector control.*
- *Air-to-ground missiles: AGM-65G Maverick, AGM-88 HARM (High-speed Anti-Radiation Missile), AGM-154C JSOW (Joint Stand-Off Weapon).*
- *Laser-guided bombs: GBU-10, GBU-12, GBU-16 and GBU-24A/B.*
- *GPS-guided munitions: GBU-31 and GBU-50 JDAM (Joint Direct Attack Munitions).*
- *Autonomous Free-flight Dispenser Systems (AFDS)*

Larissa Air Base in northern Greece is home to TAFC HQ where two Block 52+ F-16Ds assigned to 337 Squadron are shown. The aircraft nearest the camera is carrying an inert IRIS-T medium range air-to-air missile.

> The UAE contract for 80 F-16 Desert Falcons signed in March 2000 was estimated to be worth $6.4 billion

UAEAF Block 60 F-16E 3033 takes off from Nellis Air Force Base, Nevada, loaded with a GBU-31(V)1 JDAM for a mission during Exercise Red Flag. Richard VanderMeulen

progress and learned all they could about the aircraft and its capabilities. Meanwhile, the UAE's two air bases, Al Dhafra and Minhad, were upgraded and modernised to cope with the delivery of the Block 60 aircraft.

Part of the support facilities built was a $50 million Block 60 training system which was commissioned on July 18, 2000. The facility included weapon systems trainers (including a visual dome-type system) used by pilots, augmented by trainers with a 150 x 40° visual system for unit-level training. These include a dedicated brief and debrief station incorporating a unique mission-recording feature. The training system's components also interface with those used by the UAE's Mirage 2000-9s.

MAIDEN FLIGHT AND SERVICE INTRODUCTION

Formal radar acceptance tests were conducted in mid-July 2003 and the first APG-80 radar was delivered to Lockheed Martin by the end of September for installation in the first Block 60 F-16 airframe.

The maiden flight was originally scheduled for late November 2003, but actually took place on December 6, with Lockheed Martin chief test pilot Steve Barter at the controls.

Former Mirage 2000 and Hawk pilots were the first to arrive at Arizona Air National Guard's 162nd Fighter Wing (FW) based at Tucson Air National Guard Base in 2001. Their F-16 conversion training started immediately using US Air Force F-16s. Conversion to the F-16 was the primary element of the training, but the 162nd FW also aimed to train the UAE fighter pilots as capable coalition warfighters.

The 162nd FW received the first two of 15 Block 60 F-16s on September 3, 2004. Pilot training on the F-16F started that month and the first cadre of UAE pilots completed their course in April 2005.

The first six Desert Falcons were flown from Lockheed Martin's Fort Worth plant to the UAE by the newly graduated pilots at the end of April 2005. They arrived at Al Dhafra Air Base on May 3 where they were greeted by the Crown Prince, Sheikh Mohammed bin Zayed Al Nahyan, Deputy Supreme Commander of the UAE Armed Forces, and assigned to the newly activated 16 Squadron.

A decision was soon taken that UAEAF F-16 squadrons would be numbered in sequence starting with 1 Squadron, which was operating the Mirage 2000 and Hawk at the time. It took 24 months for the squadron to be renumbered as 1 Squadron: its Mirages and Hawks were dispersed to other units.

Under original plans, the Emirati F-16s were originally expected to equip a squadron at Al Dhafra (part of Western Air Command – the former Abu Dhabi Air Force) first, and then a squadron at Minhad (Central Air Command - the former Dubai Air Force). In the event, all three squadrons were based at Al Dhafra, alongside 71 and 76 Squadron flying the Mirage 2000.

From June 2007, UAEAF pilots began taking a course on the introduction to fighter fundamentals as a precursor to Block 60 F-16 conversion training. Instruction was provided by the Alliance Aviation Center of Excellence and Lockheed Martin Simulation, Training and Support at Alliance International Airport in Fort Worth, Texas.

It has been reported that a relatively large number of foreign (mainly Pakistani) pilots serve with the UAEAF F-16 units, but this cannot be confirmed, nor has there been any

F-16 Falcon Still in the Fight

This Block 60 F-16F carries two CATM-88 High-speed Anti Radiation Missiles. Scott Fischer

F-16E 3080 loaded with a GBU-31(V)3 JDAM converted from a 2,000lb BLU-109 penetrating warhead. Carl Richards

F-16E 3080 loaded with an AGM-65 Maverick air-to-ground missile. Carl Richards

F-16F 3001 loaded with four 2,000lb GBU-24/B Paveway III laser-guided bombs. Carl Richards

F-16F 3003 loaded with four 2,000lb GBU-15(V)2C/B GPS-guided stand-off weapons with Mk84 warheads. Scott Fischer

indication as to how these pilots were trained. This is not a unique situation. The UAEAF employs a large cadre of foreign personnel that include people from France, Jordan, New Zealand, the UK and the United States.

The UAE Air Force Desert Falcon made its public debut during the first day of the Al Ain Aerobatics show on January 11, 2006; when four F-16Es flew past in formation. Two days earlier F-16E 3052 crashed during a practice display at Al Ain. Lockheed Martin Test Pilot Dan Levin ejected safely.

A more impressive display was given at the Dubai air show in November 2007, with the aircraft being flown by a Lockheed Martin test pilot.

SMASHING ARSENAL

Efforts continued at Fort Worth to integrate more weapons on to the new variant while the UAEAF was introducing the aircraft into service. Though the Block 60's weapons fit has never been officially detailed, flight tests with different weapons were photographed at Fort Worth, mainly using F-16Fs 3001, 3002, and 3003, and F-16E 3080.

Air-to-air weapons were cleared first, with the first F-16F 3001/N161LM seen carrying dummy AIM-120 AMRAAM missiles on its December 6, 2003 maiden flight. The same aircraft was noted carrying AIM-9P Sidewinder short range air-to-air missiles on its wingtip stations in November 2004, with AMRAAMs returning in December. The aircraft began trials with air-to-ground weapons soon afterwards, photographed at Fort Worth with triple bomb racks loaded with GBU-12s with Mk82 warheads in March 2005. The aircraft was used for clearance trials of the smaller 500lb (227kg) version of GEC's Al

F-16F 3002 loaded with a Wind Corrected Munitions Dispenser on station 9 and a 2,000lb GBU-15 Electro Optical-guided stand-off weapon on station 3. Scott Fischer

Hakim modular stand-off bomb in April 2006 and later, in March 2007, was used to test a payload of four AGM-88 High-speed Anti-Radiation Missiles.

F-16F 3002 was photographed at Fort Worth in April 2006 carrying the 500lb GBU-12 Paveway II laser-guided bomb (LGB) and the AGM-88 HARM at much the same time. In August 2007 aircraft 3002 was seen at Fort Worth loaded with an unidentified weapon (probably a CBU-103/CBU-105 Wind Corrected Munitions Dispenser). The aircraft was subsequently seen carrying a version of the larger 2,000lb (907kg) Al Hakim in August 2007.

F-16F 3003 was used for testing a number of heavy weapons configurations, and was photographed carrying a 2,000lb Paveway III laser-guided bomb under each wing in September 2005. The aircraft was subsequently photographed carrying first a pair of 2,000lb class GEC Al Hakim modular air-to-surface missiles in January 2006, followed by a four-weapon fit in April. The aircraft was also used for clearance of the 2,000lb GBU-31 Joint Direct Attack Munition. Finally, single-seat F-16E 3080 was used to clear the AGM-65 Maverick air-to-ground missile in March 2007.

At one time, there seemed to be every chance the Royal Saudi Air Force would not receive the AIM-120 AMRAAM, though US objections to selling the air-to-air missile in the region dissipated in 1994, when Qatar purchased the French Mica, a beyond visual range air-to-air missile for its Mirage 2000s.

A Defense Security Cooperation Agency notification to Congress covering the supply of the AIM-120 AMRAAM was finally issued on January 3, 2008 and on February 22, 2009 Raytheon confirmed the UAE and the US Governments had issued a letter of offer and acceptance for 224 AIM-120C7s to equip UAE F-16s.

Another weapon the UAE wanted to integrate on its F-16s was the MBDA Black Shaheen air-to-surface stand-off missile. This was deemed unacceptable by the US Government and its powerful pro-Israeli lobby because the range exceeded 185 mile (300km), the defining limit for cruise missiles under the Missile Technology Control Regime. The US did not want the UAE to have access to the weapon, which was an export version of the Apache, Scalp EG and Storm Shadow. Lockheed Martin was instructed it could not change the Block 60's data bus to enable it to carry the Black Shaheen. Instead, the Emiratis simply modified some of its Mirage 2000-9s to carry the weapon.

The US did approve the UAE's request to buy enhanced GBU-12F/B Paveway dual-mode laser-guided bombs in December 2009. The GBU-12F/B enables targeting through sandstorms, fog or cloud, conditions that obstruct a laser, while retaining precision accuracy and the ability to hit moving targets once conditions allow the use of a laser.

RED FLAG, GULF RETURN AND COMBAT OPS

UAEAF F-16s participated in their first multi-national Red Flag exercise in August 2009 at Nellis Air Force Base, Nevada. Air and ground crew deployed from the UAE flew aircraft from the training element assigned to the 162nd FW at Tucson.

Just over a year later, the UAE began to wrap up its US-based training operation, and flew five of its 13 F-16s home on October 20, 2010. The remainder flew to the UAE over the following month, bringing to an end the Emirati presence at Tucson.

The UAE sent six Block 60s to participate in the international military operation to enforce United Nations Security Council Resolution 1973 in Libya in March 2011.

The aircraft arrived at Decimomannu Air Base on the Italian island of Sardinia on March 27, each carrying four AIM-120 AMRAAM and two AIM-9L Sidewinder air-to-air missiles, a

F-16F 3001 loaded with multiple 500lb GBU-12 Paveway II laser-guided bombs with Mk82 warheads. Carl Richards

F-16F 3001 loaded with four 2,000lb GBU-15(V)31A/B Electro-Optical-guided stand-off weapons with BLU-109 penetrating warheads and short chord strakes, canards and wings. Scott Fischer

centreline, under wing and conformal fuel tanks. One AMRAAM was carried on each wingtip station while the outboard underwing stations carried a twin launcher loaded with an AMRAAM (outboard) and an AIM-9L. During subsequent missions the aircraft tended to fly with underwing tanks, CFTs, two wingtip-mounted AMRAAMs, and two underwing AIM-9Ls. When the operation moved to include air strikes, the Block 60s were seen with a payload comprising four AMRAAMs, and two 500lb (227kg) GBU-12 Paveway II or Enhanced Paveway II laser-guided bombs. Unlike the Mirage 2000s also deployed, the F-16s do not seem to have carried the Al Hakim stand-off bomb.

One F-16F was lost at Naval Air Station Sigonella, Sicily, on April 27, 2011 (where the UAE detachment had moved to) when the aircraft left the runway on landing. The pilot ejected safely and the aircraft was deemed repairable.

MORE AIRCRAFT, MORE OPS

During a visit to the Persian Gulf in April 2013, US Secretary of Defense Chuck Hagel announced the UAE would obtain 25 more F-16s with a cache of unspecified stand-off weapons. The aircraft were to be purchased through a direct commercial sale, not the Foreign Military Sale (FMS) process, and would augment the existing Desert Falcon fleet. Some weapons, support equipment and services were to be supplied under an FMS sale allowing for Defense Security Cooperation Agency (DSCA) notifications to Congress associated with the deal.

In October 2013 the DSCA notified Congress of the possible supply of 300 AGM-84 SLAM-ER missiles, 1,200 AGM-154C Joint Stand-Off Weapons and 5,000 GBU-39/B Small Diameter Bombs for the UAEAF F-16 fleet, including 25 new aircraft.

By January 2014 the number of new aircraft had increased to 30 and referred to as Block 61s. The 79 Block 60 Desert Falcons already in service are to be upgraded to a similar standard and referred to as Block 60+.

The Block 61 was believed to be an evolutionary upgrade of the original Block 60 that would overcome issues with diminishing manufacturing sources and obsolescence and some interoperability enhancements, though the Block 61 deal did not materialise.

Despite the deal, the US still refused to integrate the Black Shaheen missile on the future Block 60+, nor would it supply an alternative long-range stand-off weapon

UAEAF ground crew discuss the aircraft's status with the pilot after a Red Flag mission at Nellis Air Force Base.
Richard VanderMeulen

such as the AGM-158 Joint Air to Surface Standoff Missile. Instead, the US is providing 155-mile (250km) range AGM-84 SLAM-ER missiles, and the stealthy 2,000lb (907kg) AGM-154C Joint Stand Off Weapon, a glide bomb that uses GPS for navigation and IR guidance for terminal guidance.

From September 22, 2014 UAEAF Block 60s participated in attacks against Islamic State (IS) targets in Syria under Operation Inherent Resolve: the second combat operation for the UAEAF F-16 force. The first mission was led by Major Mariam Al Mansouri, the UAE's first female fighter pilot, and an F-16 squadron commander.

UAEAF aircraft were briefly withdrawn from operations following the loss of a Royal Jordanian Air Force F-16 on December 24. The aircraft crashed seven miles (11km) east of Al-Raqqa the self-proclaimed capital of so-called Islamic State (ISIS).

Pilot, Lt Muath Safi Yousef Al Kasasbeh of No.1 Squadron, RJAF, successfully ejected but was captured and subsequently executed by Islamic State militants.

The RJAF and UAEAF continued to indirectly support the operation by providing bases for other allied aircraft, but stopped participating in air strikes, complaining that US Air Force combat search and rescue (CSAR) forces based in Kuwait were too far from the operational area.

In response to its allies' concerns, the US Air Force repositioned A-10s from Afghanistan to Kuwait, partly to support possible future CSAR missions, and a V-22 Osprey unit from Kuwait to Irbil in northern Iraq.

Once the American CSAR assets were repositioned, the UAE rejoined the air campaign and redoubled its efforts, deploying an F-16 squadron to Amman in Jordan on February 8, supported by A330 MRTT tankers and a C-17 airlift aircraft.

More recently, the UAE reportedly deployed 30 aircraft in support of Operation Decisive Storm. These included at least one A330 MRTT tanker, and a number of fighters. Desert Falcons were filmed operating from Khamis Mushayt Air Base in Saudi Arabia. Footage showed the aircraft operating with AMRAAMs, Sidewinders, either GBU-12F/B Paveways or JDAMs, and external fuel tanks on the inboard pylons.

One aircraft was named 'The Martyr Sulaiman el-Maliki', after the first Saudi soldier killed in the Saudi-led operation.

Jon Lake

Japan's HYBRID F-16

The Mitsubishi Heavy Industries F-2 fighter was designed to defeat a Soviet amphibious invasion of Japan, delivering stand-off air-to-surface missiles and guided munitions against land and sea targets defended by dense fighter and surface-to-air missile defences.

In the early 1980s, this nightmare scenario seemed

> The F-2 will remain in service until the FY2028-2030 timeline, when it is supposed to be replaced by Japan's fifth-generation F-3 stealth fighter design

Note the wing and horizontal stabiliser profiles which differ to the baseline F-16 on F-2A 03-8503 of 6 Hikotai based at Tsuiki Air Base. All images Andreas Zeitler unless noted

frighteningly close to reality. The Soviet build-up in the Far East and the 1983 shoot-down of Korean Air Lines Flight 007 brought the Cold War threat home to Japan.

The F-2 design started in the early 1980s as the FS-X, an indigenous fighter to replace the Japan Air Self-Defense Force's (JASDF) F-1 fleet, the combat version of the 1960s-design T-1 trainer and Japan's first production combat jet.

The F-2 was designed as an air-to-surface support fighter (a capability that was then considered difficult to reconcile with the JASDF's 'self-defence' mission). In addition to the operational requirement – to defeat a Soviet invasion – the FS-X programme was intended to increase the capability of Japan's aerospace industry (and national prestige) at a time when its economy was booming.

But it was soon apparent that even an indigenous design would require a US engine to produce the performance required for it to carry out its mission.

Rather than just supply an engine, the United States Government wanted Japan to buy US-built combat aircraft or, failing that, carry out-of-licence production of US designs.

Japan had already built interceptors and maritime patrol aircraft vital to Cold War defence of Japan. The licence-built fighters were used mainly as interceptors, integrated with the JASDF-specific version of the multi-service BADGE (Base Air Defence Ground Environment) system for ground

Type 93 ASM-2 electro-optical and infrared-guided anti-ship missiles.

The F-2 design started in the early 1990s as the FS-X programme, an indigenous fighter to replace the Japan Air Self-Defense Force F-1 fleet

controlled interception. (Co-ordination between different Japanese services was then also seen as politically difficult to achieve.)

Faced with the US policy goals, it was also apparent to the Japanese that it would likely be daunting (and expensive) to develop an indigenous design that would able to meet the operational and technical requirements.

After briefly considering licence-production of the European Panavia Tornado, the Japanese turned to the United States for a new fighter.

ORIGINS OF A HYBRID

The indigenous FS-X transitioned to the F-2 programme and was intended to reconcile Japan's operational needs and industrial goals with the US desire to sell an off-the-shelf design.

Japan looked at other existing American fighters, but the F-2 emerged as a hybrid (US-Japanese) niche 'support' fighter design based on the General Dynamics (GD) Block 40 F-16C/F-16D Fighting Falcon. It was the first bilateral US-Japanese development of a combat aircraft or, indeed, of any major weapons system.

After negotiations, it was decided the F-2's design and production was to be split 60:40 between Japan and the United States including US-built General Electric F110-GE-129 engines.

The partnership was established to assure access to the cutting-edge technology Japan was willing to pay to develop the F-2 despite being constitutionally unable to export the aircraft.

Both nations were unfamiliar with the additional costs and frustrations imposed by multinational aircraft programmes that Europe had been experiencing for

A GBU-54 Laser JDAM test vehicle loaded on F-2A 53-8535.

years. The F-2 had to evolve with similar understandings and work-arounds.

The Japanese insistence on incorporating advanced technology in the F-2 made it in effect a new generation jet fighter, and represented a major upgrade to the Block 40 F-16 design.

The F-2 was the first production fighter to include a major carbon-fibre composite structure in the enlarged wing design originally intended for the F-16XL Agile Falcon. The latter had been developed by GD but not produced. It was fitted with the Japanese-designed Mitsubishi Electronics J/APG-1 advanced electronically scanned array (AESA) radar, the first combat aircraft designed with an AESA radar system. It used technology developed by the Japanese Defense Agency's Technical Research and Development Institute (TRDI).

Technology transfer concerns further delayed the F-2 programme. When the United States refused to release the source code for the GD-developed fly-by-wire control system, Japan Aviation Electronics and Honeywell recreated an alternative version and tested it on a modified Mitsubishi T-2 Control Configured Vehicle (CCV). This delayed the programme for two years.

Structural problems were encountered with the adaption of the Agile Falcon's wing to the composite material used on the F-2, which was followed by wing flutter issues that caused further delays.

Large air-to-surface missiles (ASMs) required by the Japanese as armament for the support fighter mission led to cracks developing in the wings when fully loaded. Other problems were addressed only after the F-2 entered service.

As a result, the F-2, as is the case with so many combat aircraft, took more time and money (a unit cost of over $100 million) to prepare it for service than originally planned. By the time the memorandum of understanding (MoU) for production was signed in 1996 and the first F-2s were finally delivered to the JASDF in 2000, the Soviet amphibious threat had faded away. The rusted landing craft that had once belonged to the Red Banner Pacific Fleet were towed past the Japanese coast on their way to scrapyards in Asia.

THE F-2 EVOLVES

With the Soviet threat gone, the JASDF dropped its support fighter category in 2005, but the F-2s still retained the air-to-surface mission, weapon loads, and their maritime camouflage. Now, other JASDF fighters could carry out the air-to-surface mission and co-operation with other Japanese services was seen as less politically provocative.

In April 2005 the Japan Defense Agency (JDA) confirmed it had studied the offensive use of airpower against imminent threats. The F-2 made its first deployment outside Japan to Guam in June 2007 to participate in Exercise Cope North. This was the first time JASDF F-2s had employed live ordnance. It took place on the Farallon de Medinilla island range and marked the first step of an incremental upgrade of the aircraft's air-to-surface capability.

F-2 units, armed with air-to-air missiles, also started standing alert duty supplementing JASDF F-4EJ Phantoms and F-15J Eagles in intercepting foreign aircraft approaching Japanese airspace.

The F-2 programme did not end Japan's interest in indigenous fighter designs. When the US repeatedly blocked export of the Lockheed Martin F-22 Raptor to Japan, despite their willingness to buy 40 aircraft off the Marietta, Georgia production line, Japan still required an indigenous stealth design to replace the F-2. This was the case even before production ended in 2011.

Mitsubishi Heavy Industries built four prototypes and 94 production series F-2s rather than 141 originally planned (subsequently reduced to 130), reflecting the high production costs and changing operational requirements.

This was a blow to Japan's aerospace industrial base and, to keep the production line open, a proposed upgrade designated the F-2 Super Kai, was offered to the JASDF.

A mock-up was first shown at the October 2004 Japan International Aerospace exhibition in Yokohama. It incorporated a helmet-mounted sight, an improved targeting pod, conformal fuel tanks, advanced mission computers and radar

F-16 Falcon Still in the Fight

XF-2A 63-8501 loaded with two ASM-3 test vehicles landing at Gifu Air Base, home of the Air Development and Test Wing. Katsunori Kimura

improvements developed for the Block 50 F-16.

A further F-2 version was also offered powered by the F110-GE-132 engine (replacing the F110-IHI-129) with an additional 10% thrust and upgraded radar. Japanese press reports dubbed the version as the F-2 FI (fighter interceptor). Neither version was built, but radar technology development continued.

The earthquake and tsunami of March 11, 2011 hit Matsushima Air Base, home to 21 Hikotai (21st Fighter Squadron), the F-2 training and transition unit. Flooding damaged 18 two-seat F-2Bs. Of these, five were deemed beyond repair, with the remainder requiring major refurbishment to return the aircraft to service. The joint MHI-Lockheed Martin programme is costing Japan $660 million. Work on the first aircraft started in early 2014 at MHI's Komaki South plant and the first two aircraft returned to service in April 2015.

Delays within the refurbishment programme were caused by the wind-down of the production line and former suppliers having left the industrial base in the absence of orders. Once repairs are completed, the JASDF will operate 63 single-seat F-2As and 28 F-2Bs.

F-2 CHANGES

The JASDF moved its F-2 units. In 2014, it announced plans to concentrate an operational force of 40 F-2s flown by two squadrons at Tsuiki, Japan's westernmost air base on the island of Kyushu. This was implemented by moving one of the two F-2 squadrons at Misawa Air Base to Tsuiki, which made room for the first JASDF F-35 squadron.

The JASDF started work on an F-2 air-to-air capability upgrade for 60 aircraft originally announced in 2012. Nine upgrade kits were included in the budget request

The J/AAQ-2 targeting pod used by the F-2A is 2.16m long, has a fuselage diameter of 360mm and weighs 164.9kg.

F-16 Falcon Still in the Fight

Air Development and Test Wing XF-2A 63-8501 loaded with a GBU-38 JDAM test vehicle. Katsunori Kimura

> **The F-2 was designed to defeat a Soviet amphibious invasion of Japan**

announced in February 2015, which included funding for two Japan Self-Defense Force Digital Communication System (Fighter) data link systems. Abbreviated to JDCS (F), the link allows data from the Japan Aerospace Defense Ground Environment (JADGE) system to be shared with land and naval forces.

The upgrade package also includes the Mitsubishi Electronics J/APG-2 AESA radar, an advanced version of the previous upgrades proposed. In Fiscal Year 2014, 30 J/APG-2 radars were procured.

A prototype of an advanced targeting pod was built for test purposes, funded in the FY 2015 budget.

The upgraded F-2 will be capable of carrying four AAM-4B air-to-air missiles and simultaneously engage multiple targets. The AAM-4B is fitted with an active-homing AESA radar and data link. It is an improved version of the Type 99 AAM-4, which replaced the AIM-7 Sparrow beyond visual range missile when it entered JASDF service with the F-15EJ Eagle in 2007.

The JASDF has also integrated the thrust-vectoring, high off-bore sight Type 4 AAM-5 short range infrared-guided missile on to the F-2 to replace the indigenous Type 90 AAM-3 and AIM-9 Sidewinder.

Since the F-2 entered service its primary weapons have been MHI Type 93 ASM-2 and Type 96 air-to-surface missiles. Up to four of each type, or a mix of both, can be carried. Both types are being replaced with the ramjet-powered ASM-3 which is scheduled to enter service in the near future.

The F-2 was designed to carry indigenous 500lb and 750lb Japanese Mark I and Mark II bombs fitted with infrared-guidance kits. These were procured in preference to earlier-generation laser-guidance technology. The GPS-guided Joint Direct Attack Munition is integrated on the F-2 and

A Type 4 AAM-5 infrared-guided, short-range air-to-air missile on station 1 of XF-2A 63-5301.

Air Development and Test Wing XF-2A 63-5301 loaded with a GBU-38 JDAM test vehicle.

entered JASDF service in 2008.

The F-2 is also being upgraded with integral target designators with moving target capability, especially ships, for employment of the GBU-54 Laser JDAM. In 2014, the JASDF announced that F-2 squadrons will be trained to strike targets designated by ground units using laser-guided bombs. The Japanese press highlighted how this interoperability was a major advance in joint operations and a response to a new Chinese amphibious capability.

F-2 FUTURE

Combining elements of fifth-generation fighter design with the baseline fourth-generation F-16C, the F-2 emerged as a Japanese-version of the F-16XL. An evolution made difficult by the need to incorporate innovative composite wing structures and an AESA radar.

Despite having the flexibility and adaptability of the basic F-16C from which it was derived, the F-2 proved to be one of the most expensive combat aircraft of its time.

Determining whether the cost of developing the technology used in the F-2 and the associated national prestige is difficult and remains an entirely subjective exercise. While the Japanese aerospace industry emerged as one of the world's most proficient at fabricating all-composite structures – as demonstrated by its participation in the Boeing 787 Dreamliner production – how much resulted from its pioneering work on the F-2 is uncertain.

The F-2 will remain in service until the FY2028-2030 timeline, when it is supposed to be replaced by Japan's fifth-generation F-3 stealth fighter design. Replacing the F-2 is all dependent on the F-3 being ready in time, and not being economically and technologically unfeasible.

As a relatively small but high-technology force, which Japan remains willing to pay a premium for even in difficult economic times, the F-2 fits with the JASDF's posture.

The F-2 is more capable than ever with an expanded air-to-surface capability achieved by integrating improved weapons and sensors, participating in multinational exercises and interoperating with other Japanese armed services. *David C Isby*